1,000 Sayings: Famous Quotes, Foreign Phrases, and Slang You Should Know

By David A. Snively, Sr

ISBN: 979-8-9985994-1-5

Snively & Co. Publishing
Printed on demand in the United States of America
For permissions or inquiries: Snively & Co Publishing

I0025620

Dedication

To my son David (Jr.) and my daughter Jennifer; to my grandchildren Alexa, Aden, Hailey, Connor, and Olivia; and to my great-grandchildren Presley, Lennon, and Harper.

You are my legacy, my laughter, and my love

FOREWORD

I've spent my life surrounded by people who know something about everything—and others who think they do. The difference, I've learned, isn't education or ego. It's curiosity. The ones worth listening to aren't the loudest; they're the ones still asking questions long after the shouting stops.

This book was born from that idea. The world rewards confidence, but confidence means nothing without understanding. So these pages are a toolkit: short, sharp insights designed to help you hold your own in any conversation—without becoming "that person" everyone avoids at dinner.

My family has been the quiet heartbeat behind every word here. My son and daughter, who remind me every day that curiosity is inherited, not taught. And the rest of my family, whose stories and humor keep me humble enough to keep learning. They've each contributed to the way I see the world—and to why I want others to see it a little clearer, too.

If you're holding this book, you already belong to that tribe of thinkers who'd rather light a spark than start a fire. Read a few lines. Let them sit. Drop them into a conversation someday and watch what happens.

"If you're right, there's no need to yell. And if you're wrong, you can't afford to."

About the Author

David Allen Snively, Sr. is a lifelong seeker of knowledge and a passionate writer dedicated to sharing wisdom with the world. With a background in education, communication, and a love for language, he has compiled numerous collections that aim to educate, entertain, and inspire. When he's not writing, he can be found exploring nature, studying languages, and mentoring others to unlock their creative voices.

Acknowledgments

This book could not have been completed without the encouragement, laughter, and wisdom of those around me. To my friends, my loved ones, and those who challenged me to keep writing—thank you.

Special thanks to the great thinkers of the past and present, whose words form the foundation of this collection.

And to the reader: thank you for choosing this book. May it remind you that words still matter.

Chapter 1: Common Everyday Sayings

1. Actions speak louder than words
Meaning: What people do is more important than what they say.
Origin: Proverb (English)

2. The early bird catches the worm
Meaning: Success comes to those who prepare well and put in effort early.
Origin: Proverb (English)

3. Honesty is the best policy
Meaning: Telling the truth is always the best approach.
Origin: Benjamin Franklin.

4. A picture is worth a thousand words
Meaning: Visuals can convey more meaning than descriptions.
Origin: Chinese Proverb.

5. Practice makes perfect
Meaning: Repeated practice leads to improvement.
Origin: Latin Proverb.

6. Don't cry over spilled milk
Meaning: Don't waste time worrying about things that can't be changed.
Origin: Proverb (English)

7. Bite the bullet
Meaning: To endure a painful or difficult situation bravely.
Origin: Military origin.

8. Better late than never
Meaning: It's better to do something late than not at all.
Origin: Proverb (English)

9. Every cloud has a silver lining
Meaning: Even bad situations have positive aspects.
Origin: John Milton, 17th century.

10. Break a leg
Meaning: A way to wish someone good luck.
Origin: Theatrical superstition.

11. Hit the nail on the head
Meaning: To describe exactly what is causing a situation or problem.
Origin: Carpentry expression.

12. Rome wasn't built in a day
Meaning: Important things take time to develop.
Origin: French Proverb, 12th century.

13. The grass is always greener on the other side
Meaning: People tend to desire what they don't have.
Origin: Proverb (English)

14. You can't judge a book by its cover
Meaning: Don't make assumptions based on appearances.
Origin: Proverb (English)

15. The ball is in your court
Meaning: It's your turn to take action.
Origin: Tennis reference.

16. Don't put all your eggs in one basket
Meaning: Don't risk everything on a single opportunity.
Origin: Spanish Proverb.

17. Burning the midnight oil
Meaning: Working late into the night.
Origin: 17th-century phrase referencing oil lamps.

18. blessing in disguise
Meaning: Something that seems bad at first but turns out to be good.
Origin: Proverb (English)

19. Birds of a feather flock together
Meaning: People with similar interests tend
to associate with each other.
Origin: Latin Proverb.

20. Haste makes waste
Meaning: Rushing things leads to mistakes.
Origin: Proverb (English)

21. A penny for your thoughts
Meaning: A way to ask someone what they're thinking.
Origin: 16th-century English phrase.

22. Let sleeping dogs lie
Meaning: Avoid interfering in a situation that could cause trouble.
Origin: Scottish Proverb.

23. Many hands make light work
Meaning: Tasks become easier when shared.
Origin: Proverb (English)

24. Too many cooks spoil the broth
Meaning: Too many people involved in a task can ruin it.
Origin: Proverb (English)

25. Out of sight, out of mind
Meaning: If you don't see something, you may forget about it.
Origin: Proverb (English)

26. Look before you leap
Meaning: Consider the consequences before taking action.
Origin: Aesop's Fables.

27. No pain, no gain
Meaning: Success requires hard work and effort.
Origin: Fitness culture, 1500s origins.

28. A fool and his money are soon parted
Meaning: Foolish people are careless with their finances.
Origin: Proverb (English)

29. When in Rome, do as the Romans do
Meaning: Follow local customs when in a different place.
Origin: St. Ambrose, 4th century.

30. All's fair in love and war
Meaning: In extreme situations, normal rules don't apply.
Origin: John Lyly, 16th century.

31. If it ain't broke, don't fix it
Meaning: Don't change something that works fine.
Origin: American Proverb, 20th century.

32. Keep your chin up
Meaning: Stay positive and optimistic.
Origin: Proverb (English)

33. No use crying over spilled milk
Meaning: Don't stress over what can't be undone.
Origin: Proverb (English)

34. Throw caution to the wind
Meaning: Take a risk without worrying about the consequences.
Origin: Proverb (English)

35. Jump on the bandwagon
Meaning: Join a popular trend.
Origin: American 19th-century politics.

36. The squeaky wheel gets the grease
Meaning: People who complain get attention.
Origin: American Proverb.

37. Beggars can't be choosers
Meaning: Accept what is available, rather than being picky.
Origin: Proverb (English)

38. Don't count your chickens before they hatch
Meaning: Don't assume success before it happens.
Origin: Aesop's Fables.

39. Two heads are better than one
Meaning: Collaboration leads to better results.
Origin: John Heywood, 16th century.

40. Curiosity killed the cat
Meaning: Being too curious can lead to trouble.
Origin: Proverb (English)

41. A rolling stone gathers no moss
Meaning: A person who doesn't settle down avoids responsibilities.
Origin: Latin Proverb, 1st century BC.

42. Actions speak louder than words
Meaning: What people do is more important than what they say.
Origin: Proverb (English)

43. An apple a day keeps the doctor away
Meaning: Healthy habits prevent illness.
Origin: Proverb (English)

44. The devil is in the details
Meaning: Small details matter the most.
Origin: German Proverb.

45. Don't bite the hand that feeds you
Meaning: Don't harm those who help you.
Origin: Proverb (English)

46. You reap what you sow
Meaning: Your actions determine your results.
Origin: Biblical (reference)

47. A watched pot never boils
Meaning: Waiting impatiently makes time feel longer.
Origin: Benjamin Franklin, 18th century.

48. There's no time like the present
Meaning: Now is the best time to act.
Origin: Proverb (English)

49. Let the cat out of the bag
Meaning: To reveal a secret unintentionally.
Origin: Proverb (English)

50. The proof is in the pudding
Meaning: Results speak louder than promises.
Origin: Proverb (English)

End of Chapter 1

Chapter 2 Old Fashion Wisdom

1. A stitch in time saves nine
Meaning: Fixing a small problem early
prevents it from becoming bigger.
Origin: Proverb (English)

2. Waste not, want not
Meaning: If you don't waste resources, you won't lack them later.
Origin: Proverb (English)

3. The squeaky wheel gets the grease
Meaning: People who complain the most get attention.
Origin: American Proverb.

4. You can't make an omelet without breaking a few eggs
Meaning: Progress often requires sacrifice.
Origin: French Proverb.

5. A penny saved is a penny earned
Meaning: Saving money is just as important as earning it
Origin: Benjamin Franklin, 18th century.

6. A rolling stone gathers no moss
Meaning: Constant movement prevents responsibilities
from accumulating.
Origin: Latin Proverb, 1st century BC.

7. Measure twice, cut once
Meaning: Plan carefully before taking action.
Origin: Carpentry Proverb.

8. Don't throw the baby out with the bathwater
Meaning: Don't discard valuable things along with unwanted ones.
Origin: German Proverb, 16th century.

9. Look before you leap
Meaning: Think carefully before making a decision.
Origin: Aesop's Fables.

10. Might makes right
Meaning: Powerful people often impose their will.
Origin: Ancient Greek Philosophy.

11. Give credit where credit is due
Meaning: Recognize those who deserve recognition.
Origin: Proverb (English)

12. People who live in glass houses shouldn't throw stones
Meaning: Don't criticize others if you have flaws yourself.
Origin: Proverb (English)

13. A leopard never changes its spots
Meaning: People don't change their true nature.
Origin: Biblical (reference)

14. Too many cooks spoil the broth
Meaning: Too many people involved in a task can ruin it.
Origin: Proverb (English)

15. Do unto others as you would have them do unto you
Meaning: Treat others the way you want to be treated.
Origin: Biblical (reference)

16. He who hesitates is lost
Meaning: Delaying action can result in missed opportunities.
Origin: Proverb (English)

17. All good things must come to an end
Meaning: Nothing lasts forever.
Origin: Geoffrey Chaucer, 14th century.

18. If it ain't broke, don't fix it
Meaning: Don't change something that works fine.
Origin: American Proverb, 20th century.

19. Good things come to those who wait
Meaning: Patience leads to rewards.
Origin: Proverb (English)

20. When one door closes, another opens
Meaning: Opportunities arise from setbacks.
Origin: Alexander Graham Bell, 19th century.

21. Hindsight is 20/20
Meaning: It's easier to understand things after they happen.
Origin: American Proverb.

22. The bigger they are, the harder they fall
Meaning: More powerful people suffer greater consequences.
Origin: Proverb (English)

23. A watched pot never boils
Meaning: Time feels longer when you're waiting.
Origin: Benjamin Franklin, 18th century.

24.Jack of all trades, master of none
Meaning: Someone who dabbles in many skills often lacks expertise in any.
Origin: Proverb (English)

25.The grass is always greener on the other side
Meaning: People tend to desire what they don't have.
Origin: Proverb (English)

26.Birds of a feather flock together
Meaning: People with similar interests associate with each other.
Origin: Latin Proverb.

27.One man's trash is another man's treasure
Meaning: What's worthless to one person may be valuable to another.
Origin: Proverb (English)

28.A chain is only as strong as its weakest link
Meaning: A group is only as strong as its weakest member.
Origin: Proverb (English)

29.What goes around comes around
Meaning: Your actions will eventually return to you.
Origin: Karma-related proverb.

30.The road to hell is paved with good intentions
Meaning: Good intentions without action can lead to failure.
Origin: Proverb (English)

31.A bird in the hand is worth two in the bush
Meaning: Having something for certain is better than taking a risk.
Origin: Proverb (English)

32. Keep your friends close and your enemies closer
Meaning: Stay aware of your enemies.
Origin: Sun Tzu, The Art of War, 5th century BC.

33. Rome wasn't built in a day
Meaning: Great things take time to develop.
Origin: French Proverb, 12th century.

34. Curiosity killed the cat
Meaning: Being too curious can lead to trouble.
Origin: Proverb (English)

35. Fortune favors the bold
Meaning: Courage leads to success.
Origin: Latin Proverb.

36. Let bygones be bygones
Meaning: Forgive and move on.
Origin: Proverb (English)

37. You reap what you sow
Meaning: Your actions determine your results.
Origin: Biblical (reference)

38. A trouble shared is a trouble halved
Meaning: Talking about problems helps ease the burden
Origin: Scottish Proverb.

39. Better safe than sorry
Meaning: It's wise to be cautious.
Origin: Proverb (English)

40. Money doesn't grow on trees
Meaning: Money is valuable and should not be wasted.
Origin: American Proverb.

41. Where there's smoke, there's fire
Meaning: Rumors often have some truth.
Origin: Latin Proverb.

42. A rising tide lifts all boats
Meaning: When the economy improves, everyone benefits.
Origin: John F. Kennedy, 20th century.

43. Don't put the cart before the horse
Meaning: Don't do things in the wrong order.
Origin: Latin Proverb.

44. A penny for your thoughts
Meaning: A way to ask someone what they're thinking.
Origin: Proverb (English)

45. The devil is in the details
Meaning: Small details matter the most.
Origin: German Proverb.

46. The early bird catches the worm
Meaning: Success comes to those who prepare early.
Origin: Proverb (English)

47. Don't judge a book by its cover
Meaning: Don't make assumptions based on appearances.
Origin: Proverb (English)

48. The more things change, the more they stay the same
Meaning: Despite differences over time, some things remain constant.
Origin: French Proverb.

49. You can't have your cake and eat it too
Meaning: You can't have everything you want without compromise.
Origin: Proverb (English)

50.Lightning never strikes the same place twice

Meaning: Rare events don't happen repeatedly.
Origin: Proverb (English)

End of Chapter 2

Chapter 3: Sayings About Money

1. Money doesn't grow on trees
Meaning: Money is valuable and should not be wasted.
Origin: American Proverb.

2. Time is money
Meaning: Time is valuable and should not be wasted.
Origin: Benjamin Franklin, 18th century.

3. The best things in life are free
Meaning: Happiness comes from things that don't cost money.
Origin: Proverb (English)

4. Penny wise, pound foolish
Meaning: Being careful with small expenses while ignoring big losses.
Origin: Proverb (English)

5. A penny saved is a penny earned
Meaning: Saving money is just as important as earning it.
 Origin: Benjamin Franklin, 18th century.

6. You have to spend money to make money
Meaning:Investment are necessary to make a profit
Origin: Business Proverb

7. The rich get richer and the poor get poorer
Meaning: Wealth accumulates among the wealthy, while the poor struggle.
Origin: Economic theory.

8. Money talks
Meaning: Wealth influences decisions and actions.
Origin: Proverb (English)

9. The love of money is the root of all evil
Meaning: Greed leads to corruption.
Origin: Biblical (reference)

10. Put your money where your mouth is
Meaning: Support your claims with financial action.
Origin: American Proverb.

11. Cash is king
Meaning: Having liquid money is more valuable than assets.
Origin: Financial saying.

12. Cut your coat according to your cloth
Meaning: Live within your financial means.
Origin: Proverb (English)

13. Save for a rainy day
Meaning: Set aside money for unexpected situations.
Origin: Proverb (English)

14. Neither a borrower nor a lender be
Meaning: Avoid lending or borrowing money.
Origin: Shakespeare, *Hamlet*.

15. Throwing good money after bad
Meaning: Continuing to invest in a failing venture.
Origin: Proverb (English)

16. A rising tide lifts all boats
Meaning: When the economy improves, everyone benefits.
Origin: John F. Kennedy, 20th century.

17.Easy come, easy go
Meaning: Money that is quickly earned is easily lost.
Origin: Proverb (English)

18.If you pay peanuts, you get monkeys
Meaning: Low wages attract unskilled workers.
Origin: Business Proverb.

19.Bad money drives out good
Meaning: Inferior currency devalues better money in circulation.
Origin: Gresham's Law, economic principle.

20.Rob Peter to pay Paul
Meaning: Taking from one source to cover another debt.
Origin: Proverb (English)

21.Living hand to mouth
Meaning: Spending all income with nothing left over.
Origin: Economic Proverb.

22. Born with a silver spoon in one's mouth
Meaning: Born into wealth and privilege.
Origin: Proverb (English)

23.A golden handshake
Meaning: A large sum of money given upon retirement.
Origin: Corporate term.

24.Money makes the world go round
Meaning: The economy drives daily life.
Origin: Proverb (English)

25.Wealth is not measured in money but in happiness
Meaning: Material wealth isn't the only measure of success.
Origin: Philosophical Proverb.

26.It takes money to make money
Meaning: You must invest to earn profits.
Origin: Business Proverb.

27.Rolling in dough
Meaning: Having a lot of money.
Origin: Slang

28. Don't throw money down the drain
Meaning: Don't waste money on useless things.
Origin: Proverb (English)

29.He who pays the piper calls the tune
Meaning: The person funding something has control over it.
Origin: Proverb (English)

30.Pay yourself first
Meaning: Prioritize saving money before spending.
Origin: Financial advice.

31.A fair day's wage for a fair day's work
Meaning: Workers should be paid fairly.
Origin: Labor movement slogan.

32.Make a quick buck
Meaning: Earn money quickly, often in a dishonest way.
Origin: Slang

33. Filthy rich
Meaning: Extremely wealthy.
Origin: Slang

34. Don't put all your eggs in one basket
Meaning: Diversify your investments.
Origin: Spanish Proverb.

35. Take care of the pennies, and the pounds will take care of themselves
Meaning: Small savings add up over time.
Origin: Proverb (English)

36. The almighty dollar
Meaning: Money holds great power.
Origin: American phrase, 19th century.

37. A poor man's riches are his friends
Meaning: Friendship is more valuable than money.
Origin: Irish Proverb.

38. Fortune favors the bold
Meaning: Taking risks leads to financial success.
Origin: Latin Proverb.

39. Tighten your belt
Meaning: Reduce expenses due to financial difficulties.
Origin: Proverb (English)

40. A penny for your thoughts
Meaning: Asking someone what they are thinking.
Origin: Proverb (English)

41. Money doesn't buy happiness
Meaning: Wealth does not guarantee joy.
Origin: Proverb (English)

42. Put all your eggs in one basket
Meaning: Investing everything in one place is risky.
Origin: Spanish Proverb.

43. Money can't buy love
Meaning: Affection can't be purchased.
Origin: Proverb (English)

44.Golden opportunity
Meaning: A rare chance for financial success.
Origin: Proverb (English)

45. Live within your means
Meaning: Spend only what you can afford.
Origin: Financial Proverb.

46. The buck stops here
Meaning: Responsibility ends with the leader.
Origin: Harry S. Truman, 20th century.

47. You can't take it with you
Meaning: Money is useless after death.
Origin: Proverb (English)

48. Easy money comes with hard lessons
Meaning: Money earned quickly is often lost just as fast.
Origin: Financial Proverb.

49. Money often costs too much
Meaning: The pursuit of wealth can come at great personal cost.
Origin: Ralph Waldo Emerson.

50. A rich man's joke is always funny
Meaning: Wealth often influences how people are treated.
Origin: Proverb (English)

End of Chapter 3

Chapter 4: Sayings About Success & Failures

1. If at first, you don't succeed, try, try again
Meaning: Persistence leads to success.
Origin: Proverb (English)

2. Rome wasn't built in a day
Meaning: Great things take time.
Origin: French Proverb.

3.Nothing ventured, nothing gained
Meaning: Taking risks is necessary for success.
Origin: Proverb (English)

4.Failure is the stepping stone to success
Meaning: Learning from mistakes leads to improvement.
Origin: Proverb (English)

5.Hard work pays off
Meaning: Effort leads to rewards.
Origin: Proverb (English)

6.Go big or go home
Meaning: Commit fully to your goals.
Origin: American Saying.

7.The road to success is always under construction
Meaning: Success requires ongoing effort.
Origin: American Proverb.

8. Success is a journey, not a destination

Meaning: Success requires continuous effort.
strength

9. The only place where success comes before work is in the dictionary

Meaning: Hard work is needed for success.
Origin: Vidal Sassoon.

10. Dream big, work hard

Meaning: Ambition combined with effort leads to success.
Origin: Motivational Quote.

11. You miss 100% of the shots you don't take

Meaning: Opportunities must be seized to succeed.
Origin: Wayne Gretzky.

12. Success is not final, failure is not fatal

Meaning: Both success and failure are part of life.
Origin: Winston Churchill.

13. A winner is just a loser who tried one more time

Meaning: Success comes from persistence.
Origin: American Motivational Saying.

14. Fortune favors the bold

Meaning: Courage leads to great achievements.
Origin: Latin Proverb.

15. Winners never quit, and quitters never win

Meaning: Persistence is key to success.
Origin: Vince Lombardi.

16. Don't count your chickens before they hatch
Meaning: Don't assume success before it happens.
Origin: Aesop's Fables.

17. Aim for the moon. If you miss, you may hit a star
Meaning: Set ambitious goals.
Origin: Norman Vincent Peale.

18. He who dares wins
Meaning: Courage leads to rewards.
Origin: British SAS Motto.

19. Success breeds success
Meaning: Achieving something increases confidence for more achievements.
Origin: American Saying.

20. Fall seven times, stand up eight
Meaning: Resilience leads to victory.
Origin: Proverb (Japanese)

21. Don't put all your eggs in one basket
Meaning: Diversify your efforts to reduce risk.
Origin: Spanish Proverb.

22. Opportunity knocks but once
Meaning: Seize chances when they come.
Origin: American Proverb.

23. Act as if it were impossible to fail
Meaning: Confidence leads to success.
Origin: Dorothea Brande.

24. Big results require big ambitions
Meaning: Great success requires great goals.
Origin: Heraclitus.

25. Success doesn't come to you; you go to it
Meaning: Effort is needed to achieve goals.
Origin: Marva Collins.

26. If opportunity doesn't knock, build a door
Meaning: Create your own opportunities.
Origin: Milton Berle

27. Success is how high you bounce when you hit bottom
Meaning: Resilience determines success.
Origin: George S. Patton.

28. What doesn't kill you makes you stronger
Meaning: Hardships build resilience.
Origin: Friedrich Nietzsche.

29. Champions keep playing until they get it right
Meaning: Perseverance leads to excellence.
Origin: Billie Jean King.

30. Do what you love, and you'll never work a day in your life
Meaning: Passion makes work enjoyable.
Origin: Confucius.

31. Obstacles are those frightful things you see when you take your eyes off your goal
Meaning: Stay focused.
Origin: Henry Ford.

32. The only limit to our realization of tomorrow is our doubts of today

Meaning: Believe in possibilities.
Origin: Franklin D. Roosevelt.

33. Success consists of going from failure to failure without loss of enthusiasm

Meaning: Persistence is key.
Origin: Winston Churchill.

34.The harder you work, the luckier you get

Meaning: Effort increases success chances.
Origin: Thomas Jefferson.

35.Perseverance conquers all things

Meaning: Consistency leads to achievements.
Origin: Virgil. a

36.There are no shortcuts to any place worth going

Meaning: Success requires effort.
Origin: Beverly Sills.

37. It always seems impossible until it's done

Meaning: Difficult things become possible.
Origin: Nelson Mandela.

38. Success usually comes to those too busy to be looking for it

Meaning: Hard work brings success.
Origin: Henry David Thoreau.

39. You can't have a million-dollar dream with a minimum-wage work ethic

Meaning: Effort must match ambition.
Origin: Stephen C. Hogan.

40. Behind every success, there's a lot of unsuccessful years

Meaning: Success is built over time.
Origin: Bob Brown.

41. You learn more from failure than from success

Meaning: Failures provide valuable lessons.
Origin: Henry Ford.

42. A journey of a thousand miles begins with a single step

Meaning: Every achievement starts small
Origin: Lao Tzu

43. Believe you can, and you're halfway there

Meaning: Confidence is key to success
Origin: Theodore Roosevelt

44. Success isn't about luck, it's about preparation

Meaning: Hard work leads to results.
Origin: Colin Powell.

45. Success is simple. Do what's right, the right way, at the right time

Meaning: Execution is crucial.
Origin: Arnold H. Glasow.

46. Sometimes, the only way to win is to refuse to play
Meaning: Avoid unnecessary battles.
Origin: American Saying.

47. Success is not in what you have, but who you are
Meaning: Character defines success.
Origin: Bo Bennett.

48. Make each day your masterpiece
Meaning: Put your best effort into every day.
Origin: John Wooden.

49. Additional unique saying
Meaning: Placeholder meaning.
Origin: Placeholder origin.

50. Additional unique saying
Meaning: Placeholder meaning.
Origin: Placeholder origin.

End of Chapter 4

Chapter 5: Sayings About Life & Death

1. Live every day as if it were your last
Meaning: Life is precious and should not be wasted.
Origin: Marcus Aurelius.

2. Death is the great equalizer
Meaning: Everyone, rich or poor, meets the same fate in death.
Origin: Proverb (English)

3. You only live once (YOLO)
Meaning: Life should be lived to the fullest.
Origin: Slang

4. Memento mori
Meaning: Remember that you will die, so live wisely.
Origin: Latin Proverb, Stoic Philosophy.

5. What doesn't kill you makes you stronger
Meaning: Overcoming challenges builds resilience.
Origin: Friedrich Nietzsche.

6. The good die young
Meaning: Virtuous people often pass away too soon.
Origin: Proverb (English)

7. Life is what happens when you're busy making other plans
Meaning: Life is unpredictable.
Origin: John Lennon.

8. To live is to suffer, to survive is to find meaning in suffering
Meaning: Life is full of hardship, but we must find purpose.
Origin: Friedrich Nietzsche.

9. Death leaves a heartache no one can heal, love leaves a memory no one can steal
Meaning: Grief is deep, but love leaves lasting memories. Origin: Irish Proverb.

10. Life is short, art is long
Meaning: Time is limited, but human creations can last forever.
Origin: Hippocrates, Ancient Greece.

11. The only certainty in life is death and taxes
Meaning: Few things in life are guaranteed.
Origin: Benjamin Franklin.

12. Live and let die
Meaning: Accept that some things must end for new things to begin.
Origin: James Bond Theme Song.

13. A coward dies a thousand deaths, a hero dies but once
Meaning: Fearful people suffer repeatedly, while the brave face fate head-on.
Origin: Shakespeare, *Julius Caesar*.

14. Live each day like it's your last, but plan for tomorrow
Meaning: Balance living in the moment with preparing for the future.
Origin: Modern Proverb.

15.Do not go gentle into that good night
Meaning: Resist death with strength and courage.
Origin: Dylan Thomas, Poem.

16.Every man dies, not every man truly lives
Meaning: Life is meant to be experienced fully.
Origin: William Wallace, *Braveheart*.

17.The fear of death follows from the fear of life
Meaning: Those who fear life also fear its end.
Origin: Mark Twain.

18.A person dies twice—once when their heart stops, and again when their name is spoken for the last time
Meaning: Legacy keeps people alive in memory.
Origin: Mexican Proverb.

19.Ashes to ashes, dust to dust
Meaning: A biblical reference to the cycle of life and death.
Origin: Book of Common Prayer.

20.You can't take it with you
Meaning: Material possessions are meaningless after death.
Origin: Proverb (English)

21.He who has a why to live can bear almost any how
Meaning: Purpose gives strength in adversity.
Origin: Friedrich Nietzsche.

22.Carpe diem (Seize the day)
Meaning: Live life to the fullest while you can.
Origin: Latin Proverb, Horace.

23. When one door closes, another opens
Meaning: Opportunities arise even in loss.
Origin: Alexander Graham Bell.

24. The journey of a thousand miles begins with a single step
Meaning: Life's challenges begin with small actions.
Origin: Lao Tzu.

25. No one here gets out alive
Meaning: Life is temporary; make the most of it.
Origin: Jim Morrison.

26. Life is not measured by the number of breaths we take, but by the moments that take our breath away
Meaning: Memorable experiences define life.
Origin: Anonymous.

27. A life well lived leaves behind love and laughter
Meaning: A meaningful life impacts others positively.
Origin: Proverb.

28. Don't count the days, make the days count
Meaning: Make every moment meaningful.
Origin: Muhammad Ali.

29. Old age is like everything else.
To make a success of it, you've got to start young
Meaning: A long and fulfilling life requires early effort.
Origin: Theodore Roosevelt.

30. The best way to predict your future is to create it
Meaning: Your actions shape your destiny.
Origin: Abraham Lincoln.

31. Sometimes, we must let go of the life we have planned, to accept the life waiting for us
Meaning: Life doesn't always follow our expectations.
Origin: Joseph Campbell.

32. Live in the sunshine, swim in the sea, drink the wild air
Meaning: Embrace nature and freedom.
Origin: Ralph Waldo Emerson.

33. The meaning of life is to find your gift; the purpose of life is to give it away
Meaning: We must use our talents to help others.
Origin: Pablo Picasso.

34. Life isn't about waiting for the storm to pass, but learning to dance in the rain
Meaning: Embrace challenges rather than avoiding them.
Origin: Vivian Greene.

35. No one is actually dead until the ripples they cause in the world fade away
Meaning: Our impact on others lives on after us.
Origin: Terry Pratchett.

36. To the well-organized mind, death is but the next great adventure
Meaning: Death is not to be feared if one has lived well.
Origin: J.K. Rowling, *Harry Potter*.

37. A wise man learns more from a foolish question than a fool learns from a wise answer

Meaning: Wisdom comes from curiosity.
Origin: Bruce Lee.

38. Life is like riding a bicycle. To keep your balance, you must keep moving

Meaning: Progress requires persistence.
Origin: Albert Einstein.

39. We make a living by what we get, but we make a life by what we give

Meaning: True fulfillment comes from giving.
Origin: Winston Churchill.

40. Life is either a daring adventure or nothing at all

Meaning: Take risks and embrace challenges.
Origin: Helen Keller.

41. Life is 10% what happens to us and 90% how we react to it

Meaning: Our perspective shapes our experiences.
Origin: Charles Swindoll.

42. To love and be loved is to feel the sun from both sides

Meaning: Love is one of life's greatest joys.
Origin: David Viscott.

43. We do not remember days, we remember moments

Meaning: Life's most meaningful times are in small moments.
Origin: Cesare Pavese.

44. Life shrinks or expands in proportion to one's courage

Meaning: Fear limits us, while bravery opens possibilities.
Origin: Anaïs Nin.

45. Happiness is not something ready-made. It comes from your own actions

Meaning: Happiness is a choice we make daily.
Origin: Dalai Lama.

46. Live for yourself and you will live in vain; live for others and you will live again

Meaning: A selfless life has greater meaning.
Origin: Bob Marley.

47. To love another person is to see the face of God

Meaning: Love is the most profound human experience.
Origin: Victor Hugo, *Les Misérables*.

48. You were given life; it is your duty to find something beautiful within it

Meaning: Appreciate and contribute to life's beauty.
Origin: Anonymous.

49.Live simply so that others may simply live
Meaning: Living with less can help others have more.
Origin: Mahatma Gandhi.

50.To die will be an awfully big adventure
Meaning: Death is another great journey of life.
Origin: J.M. Barrie, *Peter Pan*.

End of Chapter 5

Chapter 6: Sayings About Family & Relationships

1.Blood is thicker than water
Meaning: Family bonds are stronger than friendships.
Origin: German Proverb.

2.Family is not an important thing, it's everything
Meaning: Family is the foundation of life.
Origin: Michael J. Fox.

3.Love makes a house a home
Meaning: A home is more than a building—it is built with love.
Origin: Proverb (English)

4.A happy family is but an earlier heaven
Meaning: A loving family brings joy.
Origin: George Bernard Shaw.

5.Charity begins at home
Meaning: One should care for their family before helping others.
Origin: Proverb (English)

6.Like father, like son
Meaning: Children often resemble their parents.
Origin: Proverb (English)

7. The apple doesn't fall far from the tree
Meaning: Children inherit traits from their parents.
Origin: European Proverb.

8.It takes a village to raise a child
Meaning: A community plays a role in a child's upbringing
.Origin: African Proverb.

9.A mother's love knows no bounds
Meaning: A mother's care is limitless.
Origin: Universal Proverb.

10. You can't choose your family
Meaning: Family is given, not chosen.
Origin: Proverb (English)

11.Home is where the heart is
Meaning: A home is about love, not location.
Origin: Pliny the Elder, Ancient Rome.

12.No man is an island
Meaning: People need connections to thrive.
Origin: John Donne.

13.Old friends are like family
Meaning: Long-term friendships are just as valuable as
family.
Origin: Proverb (English)

14.Siblings are the best friends you can't get rid of
Meaning: Brothers and sisters are lifelong companions.
Origin: Unknown

15. When you teach your son, you teach your son's son

Meaning: Lessons passed down impact generations.
Origin: Jewish Proverb.

16. A father carries pictures where his money used to be

Meaning: Parenthood is financially demanding but rewarding.
Origin: Anonymous.

17. An ounce of blood is worth more than a pound of friendship

Meaning: Family loyalty surpasses friendships.
Origin: Spanish Proverb.

18. Parents are the bones on which children sharpen their teeth

Meaning: Children grow by learning from their parents.
Origin: Peter Ustinov.

19. The best thing to hold onto in life is each other

Meaning: Family and relationships bring true happiness.
Origin: Audrey Hepburn.

20. Blood makes you related, loyalty makes you family

Meaning: Being family is about actions, not just genetics.
Origin: Unknown

21. The strength of a family lies in its love and unity

Meaning: Family unity is the key to happiness.
Origin: Universal Wisdom.

22. A house is built by hands, but a home is built by heart
Meaning: Love makes a house a home.
Origin: Proverb (English)

23. To us, family means putting your arms around each other and being there
Meaning: Family is about presence and support.
Origin: Barbara Bush.

24. A mother understands what a child does not say
Meaning: Mothers instinctively understand their children.
Origin: Jewish Proverb.

25. Happiness is having a large, loving, caring, close-knit family… in another city
Meaning: Families can be both supportive and overwhelming.
 Origin: George Burns.

26. Spending time with family is worth every second
Meaning: Family moments are precious.
Origin: Unknown

27. The love of a family is life's greatest blessing
Meaning: Family love is invaluable.
Origin: Unknown

28. Home is not a place, it's a feeling
Meaning: A home is defined by warmth and love.
Origin: Cecelia Ahern.

29. The most important thing in the world is family and love
Meaning: Family should always come first.
Origin: John Wooden.

30. Children are the anchors that hold a mother to life
Meaning: Mothers are deeply connected to their children.
Origin: Sophocles.

31. Sometimes, the smallest things take up the most room in your heart
Meaning: Little moments with loved ones mean the most.
Origin: Winnie the Pooh.

32. A man travels the world in search of what he needs and returns home to find it
Meaning: Home holds true happiness.
Origin: George Moore.

33. A son is a son till he takes a wife, a daughter is a daughter all of her life
Meaning: Daughters tend to stay closer to family.
Origin: Irish Proverb.

34. The love between a parent and a child is forever
Meaning: Parental love is unbreakable.
Origin: Unknown

35. Families are like branches on a tree; we grow in different directions, yet our roots remain as one
Meaning: Families remain con
Origin: Unknown

36. There's no place like home
Meaning: Nothing compares to being home.
Origin: L. Frank Baum, *The Wizard of Oz*.

37. A family that eats together, stays together
Meaning: Sharing meals strengthens family bonds.
Origin: Universal Proverb.

38. The laughter of a child is the light of a home
Meaning: Children bring joy to families.
Origin: Unknown

39. Love your family, spend time, be kind, and serve one another
Meaning: Family values are about love and service.
Origin: Unknown

40. Siblings: your only enemy you can't live without
Meaning: Sibling rivalry exists, but so docs love.
Origin: Unknown

41. The roots of a family tree begin with love
Meaning: Love is the foundation of a strong family.
Origin: Universal Wisdom.

42. To be in your children's memories tomorrow, be in their lives today
Meaning: Time spent with children is priceless.
Origin: Unknown

43. Grandparents: a little bit of parent, a little bit of teacher, and a little bit of best friend
Meaning: Grandparents play multiple roles in family.
Origin: Unknown

44. Home is where your story begins
Meaning: Family shapes your life story.
Origin: Unknown

45. The best inheritance a parent can give their children is a few minutes of their time each day
Meaning: Time is the most valuable gift.
Origin: Orlando Aloysius Battista.

46. Other things may change us, but we start and end with family
Meaning: Family remains constant despite life's changes.
Origin: Anthony Brandt.

47. Rejoice with your family in the beautiful land of life
Meaning: Enjoy time with loved ones.
Origin: Albert Einstein.

48. Family is not an important thing, it's everything
Meaning: Family provides emotional support, identity, and a sense of belonging that outweighs material success.
Origin: Michael J. Fox

49.The bond that links your true family is not one of blood, but of respect and joy in each other's

Meaning: True family is defined by mutual respect, care, and emotional connection rather than genetics alone.
Origin: Richard Bach, *Illusions* (1977).

50.What is done for love always takes place beyond good and evil

Meaning: Acts motivated by love transcend moral calculation and social judgment
Origin: Friedrich Nietzsche, *Beyond Good and Evil* (1886)

End of Chapter 6

Chapter 7: Sayings About Friendship

1.A friend in need is a friend indeed
Meaning: True friends help each other in difficult times.
Origin: Proverb (English)

2.Friendship doubles joy and divides grief
Meaning: Friends make happy moments better and sad moments easier.
Origin: Proverb (English)

3.A true friend is someone who knows all about you and still loves you
Meaning: Real friendship is unconditional.
Origin: Elbert Hubbard.

4.Friends are the family we choose
Meaning: Close friendships can be as strong as family bonds.
 Origin: Proverb.

5. Good friends are like stars; you don't always see them, but you know they're there
Meaning: True friends remain constant even when distant
Origin: Proverb.

6.A friend to all is a friend to none
Meaning: Trying to please everyone means not being a true friend.
Origin: Aristotle.

7.A real friend is one who walks in when the rest of the world walks out
Meaning: True friends stay through hard times.
Origin: Walter Winchell.

8.A good friend knows all your best stories, but a best friend has lived them with you
Meaning: Best friends experience life together.
Origin: Proverb (English)

9.True friendship comes when the silence between two people is comfortable
Meaning: Real friends don't need words to understand each other.
Origin: David Tyson Gentry.

10. Friendship isn't about who you've known the longest, but who walked in and never left
Meaning: Loyalty defines real friendship.
Origin: Proverb.

11.Walking with a friend in the dark is better than walking alone in the light
Meaning: True friends support each other through hardships.
Origin: Helen Keller.

12. A friend is one who overlooks your broken fence, and admires the flowers in your garden

Meaning: Friends see the best in you despite imperfections.
Origin: Proverb.

13. True friends are never apart, maybe in distance but never in heart

Meaning: Friendship transcends physical separation.
Origin: Proverb.

14. One loyal friend is worth ten thousand relatives

Meaning: A close friend can be more valuable than distant family.
Origin: Euripides.

15. A friend is someone who gives you total freedom to be yourself

Meaning: True friends accept you as you are.
Origin: Jim Morrison.

16. Friendship is born at that moment when one person says to another:
'What! You too? I thought I was the only one'

Meaning: Friendship starts with shared experiences.
Origin: C.S. Lewis.

17. The only way to have a friend is to be one

Meaning: Friendship requires effort from both sides.
Origin: Ralph Waldo Emerson.

18.No friendship is an accident
Meaning: Friendships are formed with purpose and meaning.
Origin: O. Henry.

19.Friendship is the golden thread that ties the heart of all the world
Meaning: True friendships connect people globally.
Origin: John Evelyn.

20.It's not what we have in life, but who we have in our life that matters
Meaning: Relationships matter more than possessions.
Origin: Unknown

21.There is nothing better than a friend, unless it is a friend with chocolate
Meaning: Good friends make life sweeter.
Origin: Linda Grayson.

22.Friendship is like a glass ornament, once it is broken, it can rarely be put back together
Meaning: Friendships should be handled with care.
Origin: Charles Kingsley.

23.Life is partly what we make it, and partly what it is made by the friends we choose
Meaning: Friends shape our experiences.
Origin: Tennessee Williams.

24. A true friend stabs you in the front
Meaning: Honest friends tell the truth, even if it hurts.
Origin: Oscar Wilde.

25. A good friend is like a four-leaf clover; hard to find and lucky to have
Meaning: True friendships are rare and valuable.
Origin: Irish Proverb.

26. An insincere and evil friend is more to be feared than a wild beast
Meaning: False friends are more dangerous than obvious enemies
Origin: Buddha.

27. Friendship is not about whom you have known the longest, it is about who came and never left your side
Meaning: Loyalty defines friendship, not duration.
Origin: Unknown

28. Friends show their love in times of trouble, not in happiness
Meaning: True friends support you during hardships.
Origin: Euripides.

29. A true friend never gets in your way unless you happen to be going down
Meaning: Real friends prevent you from making bad choices.
Origin: Arnold H. Glasow.

30. **A single rose can be my garden… a single friend, my world**
Meaning: One great friend can make all the difference.
Origin: Leo Buscaglia.

31. **To the world, you may be one person, but to one person you may be the world**
Meaning: Friends value you deeply.
Origin: Dr. Seuss.

32. **Friends are like walls; sometimes you lean on them, and sometimes it's just enough to know they are there**
Meaning: Friendship provides emotional support.
Origin: Unknown

33.A friend knows the song in my heart and sings it to me when my memory fails
Meaning: Friends remind us of who we truly are.
Origin: Donna Roberts.

34.Friendship improves happiness and abates misery by the doubling of our joy and the dividing of our grief
Meaning: Friends share our highs and lows.
Origin: Marcus Tullius Cicero.

35.Friendship is a sheltering tree
Meaning: Friends provide support and protection.
Origin: Samuel Taylor Coleridge.

36.I would rather walk with a friend in the dark, than alone in the light
Meaning: Friends make difficult times easier.
Origin: Helen Keller.

37.A day without a friend is like a pot without a single drop of honey
Meaning: Life is empty without friendship.
 Origin: Winnie the Pooh, A.A. Milne.

38.To have a friend, be a friend
Meaning: Friendship requires mutual care and effort.
Origin: Proverb (English)

39.Friends are treasures
Meaning: True friendship is invaluable.
Origin: Horace.

40.Friendship is the only cement that will ever hold the world together
Meaning: Strong friendships create a better world.
Origin: Woodrow Wilson.

41.Friendship marks a life even more deeply than love
Meaning: Friendship leaves a lasting impact on life.
Origin: Elie Wiesel.

42. Friendship is not something you learn in school, but if you haven't learned the meaning of friendship, you really haven't learned anything
Meaning: Friendship is one of life's most important lessons.
Origin: Muhammad Ali.

43.If you want to find out who's a true friend, screw up and see who's still there

Meaning: Real friends stand by you through mistakes.

Origin: Unknown

44.True friends speak the truth even when it hurts

Meaning: Real friends are honest, even when it's difficult.

Origin: Unknown

45.A true friendship refreshes the soul

Meaning: Good friendships bring happiness and peace.

Origin: Biblical (reference)

46. Friendship isn't a big thing—it's a million little things

Meaning: Friendship is built through small, meaningful moments.

Origin: Unknown

47. A friend is one who knows you and loves you just the same

Meaning: True friends accept you for who you are.

Origin: Unknown

48.The greatest gift of life is friendship

Meaning: Friendship is one of life's most valuable treasures.

Origin: Hubert H. Humphrey.

**49.Some people go to priests, others to poetry, I to my
friends**
Meaning: Friends offer comfort and wisdom.
Origin: Virginia Woolf.

**50.There is nothing on this earth more to be prized than
true friendship**
Meaning: Friendship is invaluable.
Origin: Thomas Aquinas.

End of Chapter 7

Chapter 8: Sayings About Work & Business

1. Hard work pays off
Meaning: Effort and dedication lead to rewards.
Origin: American Proverb.

2. The customer is always right
Meaning: Business success comes from prioritizing customer satisfaction.
Origin: Harry Gordon Selfridge, 20th century.

3. Work smarter, not harder
Meaning: Efficiency is more valuable than just effort.
Origin: Allan F. Mogensen, 1930s.

4. Rome wasn't built in a day
Meaning: Big achievements take time.
Origin: French Proverb, 12th century.

5. Do what you love, and you'll never work a day in your life
Meaning: Finding passion in your work makes it enjoyable.
Origin: Confucius.

6. Opportunities don't happen, you create them
Meaning: Success comes from taking action.
Origin: Chris Grosser.

7.Success is not just about making money, it's about making a difference
Meaning: Real success impacts others.
Origin: Unknown

8.The harder the struggle, the more glorious the triumph
Meaning: Difficult challenges lead to meaningful rewards.
Origin: Thomas Paine.

9.Choose a job you love, and you will never have to work a day in your life
Meaning: Passion for work makes it feel effortless.
Origin: Confucius.

10. It's not about ideas. It's about making ideas happen
Meaning: Execution is more important than just having ideas.
Origin: Scott Belsky.

11.Quality means doing it right when no one is looking
Meaning: True professionalism is consistent.
Origin: Henry Ford.

12.Genius is 1% inspiration and 99% perspiration
Meaning: Success requires hard work more than talent.
Origin: Thomas Edison.

13.I find that the harder I work, the more luck I seem to have
Meaning: Effort leads to more opportunities.
Origin: Thomas Jefferson.

14. Don't watch the clock; do what it does. Keep going
Meaning: Persistence leads to success.
Origin: Sam Levenson.

15. Business opportunities are like buses, there's always another one coming
Meaning: Opportunities are never-ending.
Origin: Richard Branson.

16.To be successful, the first thing to do is fall in love with your work
Meaning: Passion fuels success.
Origin: Sister Mary Lauretta.

17.A big business starts small
Meaning: Great companies begin with humble origins.
Origin: Richard Branson.

18.The best way to predict the future is to create it
Meaning: Success comes from actively shaping one's destiny.
Origin: Peter Drucker.

19.He who is not courageous enough to take risks will accomplish nothing in life
Meaning: Risk-taking is essential for success.
Origin: Muhammad Ali.

20.Far and away the best prize that life offers is the chance to work hard at work worth doing
Meaning: Meaningful work is a great reward.
Origin: Theodore Roosevelt.

21.If you don't build your dream, someone will hire you to help build theirs

Meaning: Entrepreneurs create their own futures.
Origin: Tony Gaskins.

22.Failure is simply the opportunity to begin again, this time more intelligently

Meaning: Every setback is a lesson.
Origin: Henry Ford.

23.A business that makes nothing but money is a poor business

Meaning: Business should contribute positively to society.
Origin: Henry Ford.

24.There are no secrets to success. It is the result of preparation, hard work, and learning from failure

Meaning: Success is earned through effort.
Origin: Colin Powell.

25.The only place where success comes before work is in the dictionary

Meaning: Hard work always precedes success.
Origin: Vidal Sassoon.

26. Don't be busy, be productive

Meaning: Hard work should be effective and meaningful.
Origin: Tim Ferriss.

27. You can't build a reputation on what you are going to do
Meaning: Action, not plans, defines success.
Origin: Henry Ford.

28. Work until your idols become your rivals
Meaning: Achieve success that puts you on the same level as your role models.
Origin: Unknown

29. A year from now, you may wish you had started today
Meaning: Procrastination delays success.
Origin: Karen Lamb

30. A goal without a plan is just a wish
Meaning: Success requires structured planning.
Origin: Antoine de Saint-Exupéry.

31. Don't be afraid to give up the good to go for the great
Meaning: Sometimes sacrifices are needed for success.
Origin: John D. Rockefeller.

32. Growth and comfort do not coexist
Meaning: Success requires pushing beyond comfort zones.
Origin: Ginni Rometty.

33. If everything seems under control, you're not going fast enough
Meaning: Progress requires pushing limits.
Origin: Mario Andretti.

34.Don't sit down and wait for opportunities to come. Get up and make them
Meaning: Success requires proactive effort.
Origin: Madam C.J. Walker.

35.The way to get started is to quit talking and begin doing
Meaning: Action is key to success.
Origin: Walt Disney.

36.Diligence is the mother of good luck
Meaning: Success is created through effort, not chance.
Origin: Benjamin Franklin.

37.Do one thing every day that scares you
Meaning: Growth comes from challenging oneself.
Origin: Eleanor Roosevelt.

38.If you want to achieve greatness, stop asking for permission
Meaning: Success requires boldness
Origin: Unknown

39.Surround yourself with only people who are going to lift you higher
Meaning: A positive environment fosters success.
Origin: Oprah Winfrey.

40.Find a way or make one
Meaning: Persistence is key to success.
Origin: Hannibal.

41. Act as if what you do makes a difference. It does
Meaning: Every action has an impact.
Origin: William James.

42. I attribute my success to this: I never gave or took any excuse
Meaning: Personal responsibility leads to success.
Origin: Florence Nightingale.

43. It's fine to celebrate success, but it is more important to heed the lessons of failure
Meaning: Success and failure both teach valuable lessons.
Origin: Bill Gates.

44. Start where you are. Use what you have. Do what you can
Meaning: Action is more important than perfection.
Origin: Arthur Ashe.

45. Your most unhappy customers are your greatest source of learning
Meaning: Criticism can help improve businesses.
Origin: Bill Gates.

46. You don't have to be great to start, but you have to start to be great
Meaning: Taking the first step is crucial to success.
Origin: Zig Ziglar.

47.Every problem is a gift—without problems we would not grow

Meaning: Challenges lead to personal and professional growth.
Origin: Tony Robbins.

48.Hustle until you no longer have to introduce yourself

Meaning: Hard work makes you well-known.
Origin: Unknown

49. Opportunities don't knock twice

Meaning: You must take advantage of chances when they come.
Origin: Unknown

50. Success is walking from failure to failure with no loss of enthusiasm

Meaning: Persistence is key to achieving greatness.
Origin: Winston Churchill.

End of Chapter 8

1.An apple a day keeps the doctor away
Meaning: Healthy habits prevent illness.
Origin: Proverb (English)

2.Health is wealth
Meaning: Good health is more valuable than material wealth.
Origin: Proverb (English)

3.You are what you eat
Meaning: Your diet influences your health and well-being.
Origin: French Proverb.

4.Laughter is the best medicine
Meaning: A positive attitude can improve health.
Origin: Proverb (English)

5.A sound mind in a sound body
Meaning: Mental and physical health are interconnected.
Origin: Latin Proverb.

6.Prevention is better than cure
Meaning: It's better to avoid illness than to treat it.
Origin: Desiderius Erasmus, 16th century.

7.Early to bed and early to rise makes a man healthy, wealthy, and wise
Meaning: Good sleep habits lead to success.
Origin: Benjamin Franklin.

8. Eat to live, don't live to eat
Meaning: Food should sustain life, not be its focus.
Origin: Socrates.

9. Take care of your body. It's the only place you have to live
Meaning: Your health is your lifelong home.
Origin: Jim Rohn.

10. He who has health has hope, and he who has hope has everything
Meaning: Good health gives the potential for happiness.
Origin: Arabian Proverb.

11. Good health and good sense are two of life's greatest blessings
Meaning: Health and wisdom go hand in hand.
Origin: Publilius Syrus.

12. The greatest wealth is health
Meaning: Being healthy is more valuable than money.
Origin: Virgil.

13. The best doctor gives the least medicine
Meaning: Prevention is better than cure.
Origin: Benjamin Franklin.

14. A healthy outside starts from the inside
Meaning: Well-being begins with proper self-care.
Origin: Robert Urich.

15. Your body hears everything your mind says
Meaning: Mental thoughts affect physical health.
Origin: Naomi Judd.

16. If you don't take care of your body, where are you going to live?
Meaning: Your body is your lifelong home.
Origin: Unknown

17.Wellness is the complete integration of body, mind, and spirit
Meaning: Health is more than just physical fitness.
Origin: Greg Anderson.

18.Happiness is the highest form of health
Meaning: Mental well-being is crucial to overall health.
Origin: Dalai Lama.

19.Your health is an investment, not an expense
Meaning: Taking care of yourself is a lifelong priority.
Origin: Unknown

20.The mind and body are not separate. What affects one, affects the other
Meaning: Physical and mental health are interconnected.
Origin: Unknown

21.Every human being is the author of his own health or disease
Meaning: Health is influenced by lifestyle choices.
Origin: Buddha.

22. Health isn't about being perfect, it's about being aware
Meaning: Awareness leads to better health choices.
Origin: Unknown

23.Water, air, and cleanliness are the chief articles in my pharmacopoeia
Meaning: Simple habits like drinking water and cleanliness matter.
Origin: Napoleon Bonaparte.

24. To keep the body in good health is a duty
Meaning: Health is a responsibility, not just a benefit.
Origin: Buddha.

25. It is health that is real wealth and not pieces of gold and silver
Meaning: Health is the most valuable asset.
Origin: Mahatma Gandhi.

26. Time and health are two precious assets that we don't recognize and appreciate until they are depleted
Meaning: We often take health for granted.
Origin: Denis Waitley.

27. A good laugh and a long sleep are the best cures in the doctor's book
Meaning: Rest and joy are vital for health.
Origin: Irish Proverb.

28. Self-care is not selfish
Meaning: Taking care of yourself helps you care for others.
Origin: Unknown

29. Don't take your health for granted
Meaning: Appreciate good health before it's too late.
Origin: Unknown

30. Exercise not only changes your body, it changes your mind, attitude, and mood
Meaning: Fitness improves overall well-being.
Origin: Unknown

31.Medicine sometimes heals, often relieves, but always comforts
Meaning: Healthcare provides more than just cures.
Origin: Hippocrates.

32.The secret of getting ahead is getting started
Meaning: Progress in health starts with small actions.
Origin: Mark Twain.

33.What you eat in private, you wear in public
Meaning: Your diet has visible effects on your health.
Origin: Unknown

34.Health is like money, we never have a true idea of its value until we lose it
Meaning: We appreciate health only when it's gone.
Origin: Josh Billings.

35.He who takes medicine and neglects diet wastes the skills of the physician
Meaning: Food plays a crucial role in healing.
Origin: Chinese Proverb.

36.Sickness comes on horseback but departs on foot
Meaning: Illness comes quickly but takes time to recover.
Origin: Dutch Proverb.

37.Eat well, move daily, hydrate often, sleep lots, love your body
Meaning: A simple formula for good health.
Origin: Unknown

38.A man too busy to take care of his health is like a mechanic too busy to take care of his tools
Meaning: Neglecting health leads to breakdowns.
Origin: Spanish Proverb.

39. If you're too busy to work out, you're too busy
Meaning: Exercise should be a priority.
Origin: Unknown

40.The greatest gift you can give your family and the world is a healthy you
Meaning: Your health benefits everyone around you.
Origin: Joyce Meyer.

41.Eat food, not too much, mostly plants
Meaning: Balanced nutrition leads to better health.
Origin: Michael Pollan.

42.Movement is medicine
Meaning: Exercise is essential for good health.
Origin: Unknown

43.The groundwork of all happiness is good health
Meaning: Health is the foundation of joy.
Origin: Leigh Hunt.

44.When diet is wrong, medicine is of no use. When diet is correct, medicine is not needed
Meaning: Food is the first line of healthcare.
Origin: Ayurvedic Proverb.

45.Treat your body like a temple, not a trash can
Meaning: Your health depends on what you put into your body.
Origin: Unknown

46. Do something today that your future self will thank you for
Meaning: Healthy choices benefit you in the long run.
Origin: Unknown

47. Take care of your body. It's the only place you have to live
Meaning: Health is a lifelong investment.
Origin: Jim Rohn.

48. A stitch in time saves nine
Meaning: Taking care of small health issues prevents bigger problems
. Origin: Proverb (English)

49. Your body is your most priceless possession. Take care of it
Meaning: Good health is invaluable.
Origin: Jack LaLanne.

50. Well-being is not just the absence of disease but the presence of vitality
Meaning: True health means feeling strong and full of life.
Origin: Unknown

Chapter 10: Sayings About Time & Patience

1.Time and tide wait for no man
Meaning: Time moves forward regardless of circumstances.
Origin: Geoffrey Chaucer, 14th century.

2.Change is the only constant in life
Meaning: Life is always evolving, and nothing stays the same.
Origin: Heraclitus, 5th century BC.

3.Lost time is never found again
Meaning: Time wasted cannot be recovered.
Origin: Benjamin Franklin, 18th century.

4.Better three hours too soon than a minute too late
Meaning: Being early is always better than being late.
Origin: William Shakespeare, The Merry Wives of Windsor.

5.Seize the day (Carpe Diem)
Meaning: Make the most of the present moment.
Origin: Horace, Odes, 23 BC.

6.The early bird catches the worm
Meaning: Success comes to those who start early.
Origin: Proverb (English)

7.Old habits die hard
Meaning: It is difficult to change long-established habits.
Origin: Proverbial wisdom.

8. A rolling stone gathers no moss
Meaning: Those who keep moving don't accumulate responsibilities or attachments.
Origin: Latin Proverb, 1st century BC.

9. Make hay while the sun shines
Meaning: Take advantage of opportunities before they disappear.
Origin: Proverb (English)

10. Time heals all wounds
Meaning: Emotional pain fades with time.
Origin: Geoffrey Chaucer, 14th century.

11. What is past is prologue
Meaning: Past events set the stage for the future.
Origin: William Shakespeare, The Tempest.

12. Don't put off until tomorrow what you can do today
Meaning: Procrastination leads to unnecessary delays.
Origin: Benjamin Franklin, 18th century.

13. Every cloud has a silver lining
Meaning: Even bad situations have positive aspects.
Origin: John Milton, 17th century.

14. There's no time like the present
Meaning: Now is the best time to take action.
Origin: 16th-century proverb.

15. You can't step into the same river twice
Meaning: Everything is constantly changing.
Origin: Heraclitus, 5th century BC.

16. Rome wasn't built in a day
Meaning: Great things take time and effort.
Origin: French Proverb, 12th century.

17. This too shall pass
Meaning: Every situation, good or bad, is temporary.
Origin: Persian Proverb, 13th century.

18. An ounce of prevention is worth a pound of cure
Meaning: Preventing problems is better than fixing them later.
Origin: Benjamin Franklin, 18th century.

19. All good things must come to an end
Meaning: Nothing lasts forever.
Origin: Geoffrey Chaucer, 14th century.

20. Time flies when you're having fun
Meaning: Enjoyable moments pass quickly.
Origin: 19th-century proverb.

21. Don't count your chickens before they hatch
Meaning: Don't assume success before it happens.
Origin: Aesop's Fables, 6th century BC.

22. A watched pot never boils
Meaning: Time seems to move slower when you're waiting for something.
Origin: Benjamin Franklin, 18th century.

23. The past cannot be changed, but the future is in your hands
Meaning: You can only control what happens next.
Origin: Proverbial wisdom.

24. Nothing lasts forever
Meaning: Everything changes with time.
Origin: Proverb (English)

25. History repeats itself
Meaning: Similar events tend to happen over time.
Origin: Thucydides, 5th century BC.

26. Change begins at the end of your comfort zone
Meaning: Personal growth happens when you step beyond what's familiar.
Origin: Neale Donald Walsch, 21st century.

27. A journey of a thousand miles begins with a single step
Meaning: Big changes start with small actions.
Origin: Lao Tzu, 6th century BC.

28. Life moves pretty fast. If you don't stop and look around once in a while, you could miss it
Meaning: Appreciate the moment before it passes.
Origin: Ferris Bueller's Day Off, 20th century.

29. Time is money
Meaning: Wasting time is like wasting financial opportunities.
Origin: Benjamin Franklin, 18th century.

30. Nothing is permanent except change
Meaning: Everything in life eventually changes.
Origin: Heraclitus, 5th century BC.

31. The best time to plant a tree was 20 years ago. The second-best time is now
Meaning: It's never too late to start something.
Origin: Chinese Proverb.

32. Don't dwell on the past
Meaning: Focus on the present and future instead of regretting the past.
Origin: Proverbial wisdom.

33. Out with the old, in with the new
Meaning: Embrace change and let go of outdated things.
Origin: Proverb (English)

34. You can't turn back the clock
Meaning: Time only moves forward.
Origin: Proverb (English)

35. One today is worth two tomorrows
Meaning: What you do now matters more than what you plan for later.
Origin: Benjamin Franklin, 18th century.

36. Live each day as if it were your last
Meaning: Make the most of each day.
Origin: Marcus Aurelius, 2nd century.

37. Every new beginning comes from some other beginning's end
Meaning: All endings lead to fresh starts.
Origin: Seneca, 1st century AD.

38. Patience and time do more than strength or passion
Meaning: Steady effort achieves more than force or impulse.
Origin: Jean de La Fontaine, 17th century.

39. Time waits for no one
Meaning: Life keeps moving forward no matter what.
Origin: Proverbial wisdom.

40. He who hesitates is lost
Meaning: Delaying action can result in missed opportunities.
Origin: Joseph Addison, 18th century.

41. The future depends on what we do in the present
Meaning: Your actions today shape your tomorrow.
Origin: Mahatma Gandhi, 20th century.

42. It's never too late to be what you might have been
Meaning: You can always work toward your potential.
Origin: George Eliot, 19th century.

43. No man ever steps in the same river twice
Meaning: Life is constantly changing, even if it looks the same.
Origin: Heraclitus, 5th century BC.

44. Let go of the past and move forward
Meaning: Dwelling on the past prevents progress.
Origin: Proverbial wisdom.

45. Time brings all things to pass
Meaning: Everything changes with time, and nothing remains the same.
Origin: Aeschylus, 5th century BC.

46.The two most powerful warriors are patience and time

Meaning: Success comes to those who persist and allow time to work.
Origin: Leo Tolstoy, War and Peace, 19th century.

47.Yesterday is history, tomorrow is a mystery, but today is a gift. That is why it is called the present

Meaning: Appreciate the present moment because it's all we truly have.
Origin: Proverbial wisdom, popularized in Kung Fu Panda, 21st century.

48.Patience is bitter, but its fruit is sweet

Meaning: Patience is difficult, but the results are rewarding.
Origin: Aristotle.

49.Time is what we want most, but what we use worst

Meaning: People often waste time despite its value.
Origin: William Penn.

50.The bad news is time flies. The good news is you're the pilot

Meaning: You control how you use your time.
Origin: Michael Altshuler.

End of Chapter 10

Chapter 11: Sayings About Luck & Fate

1.Fortune favors the bold
Meaning: Luck comes to those who take risks.
Origin: Latin Proverb.

2.Luck is what happens when preparation meets opportunity
Meaning: Being ready creates good luck.
Origin: Seneca, 1st century AD

3.The harder I work, the luckier I get
Meaning: Effort increases the chances of success.
Origin: Thomas Jefferson.

4.Fate leads the willing and drags along the reluctant
Meaning: Destiny helps those who embrace it.
Origin: Seneca.

5.Some people are born lucky
Meaning: Some individuals seem to have luck from birth.
Origin: Proverb (English)

6.You make your own luck
Meaning: Hard work and persistence create luck.
Origin: Unknown

7.A stroke of luck can change everything
Meaning: Fortune can shift quickly and unexpectedly.
Origin: Unknown

8.It's better to be lucky than good
Meaning: Sometimes luck is more useful than skill.
Origin: American Saying.

9. When one door closes, another opens
Meaning: Opportunities arise when setbacks occur.
Origin: Alexander Graham Bell.

10. Third time's the charm
Meaning: Success often comes after multiple attempts.
Origin: Proverb (English)

11. The best luck of all is the luck you make for yourself
Meaning: Luck is often the result of effort.
Origin: Douglas MacArthur.

12. Luck always seems to be against the man who depends on it
Meaning: Relying on luck alone leads to failure.
Origin: Proverb (English)

13. A lucky break can be life-changing
Meaning: Unexpected fortune can bring success.
Origin: Unknown

14. Better an ounce of luck than a pound of gold
Meaning: Luck is sometimes more valuable than wealth.
Origin: Yiddish Proverb.

15. Gambling with fate is never wise
Meaning: Taking unnecessary risks can be dangerous.
Origin: Unknown

16. The wheel of fortune turns for everyone
Meaning: Luck changes over time for all.
Origin: Medieval Proverb.

17.Fortune smiles on those who act
Meaning: Taking initiative invites luck.
Origin: Unknown

18.Throwing caution to the wind can sometimes bring luck
Meaning: Taking risks can lead to unexpected rewards.
Origin: Unknown

19. Luck favors those who don't wait for it
Meaning: People who take action find more success.
Origin: Unknown

20.Fate is not satisfied with inflicting one calamity
Meaning: Bad luck can come in waves.
Origin: Proverb (Roman)

21.Everything happens for a reason
Meaning: Even misfortune has a purpose.
Origin: Unknown

22.A horseshoe over the door brings good luck
Meaning: A traditional superstition about fortune.
Origin: English Folklore.

23.Luck and misfortune are two sides of the same coin
Meaning: Fortune can change quickly.
Origin: Unknown

24.Luck runs out, but hard work never fails
Meaning: Effort is more reliable than luck.
Origin: Unknown

25.May the odds be ever in your favor
Meaning: Wishing someone good fortune.
Origin: The Hunger Games.

26.A four-leaf clover is a sign of good luck
Meaning: A traditional superstition about finding luck.
Origin: Irish Folklore.

27.Sometimes you win, sometimes you learn
Meaning: Not all losses are failures.
Origin: Unknown

28.Destiny is a matter of choice, not chance
Meaning: Fate is shaped by decisions.
Origin: William Jennings Bryan.

29.He who depends on luck will rarely succeed
Meaning: Success requires effort, not just chance.
Origin: Unknown

30.Throw a lucky penny in the fountain and make a wish
Meaning: A common superstition for luck.
Origin: Unknown

31.Bad luck comes in threes
Meaning: Misfortunes often seem to come in groups.
Origin: Old Superstition.

32.Some are born with a silver spoon in their mouth
Meaning: Some people are born into fortune.
Origin: Proverb (English)

33. You can't escape fate
Meaning: Destiny will always find you.
Origin: Greek Tragedy.

34. The dice have been cast
Meaning: A decision has been made, and fate will play out.
Origin: Julius Caesar, Ancient Rome.

35. Luck is like lightning – unpredictable and striking at random
Meaning: Luck is uncontrollable.
Origin: Unknown

36. A fool and his luck soon part
Meaning: Foolish people don't hold onto good fortune.
Origin: Proverb.

37. Good things come to those who wait
Meaning: Patience often leads to success.
Origin: Proverb (English)

38. Bad luck often brings unexpected good fortune
Meaning: Setbacks can lead to opportunities.
Origin: Unknown

39. If it weren't for bad luck, I'd have no luck at all
Meaning: Some people feel they always have bad luck.
Origin: Old Saying.

40. The stars align for those who are ready
Meaning: Being prepared increases opportunities.
Origin: Unknown

41. A rabbit's foot brings good luck
Meaning: A common superstition about luck.
Origin: American Folklore.

42.Chance favors the prepared mind
Meaning: Those who are ready seize opportunities.
Origin: Louis Pasteur.

43.A black cat crossing your path is bad luck
Meaning: A long-held superstition about misfortune.
Origin: European Folklore.

44.No great success was ever achieved without a little bit of luck
Meaning: Even the best need some luck.
Origin: Unknown

45.Fate whispers to the warrior, 'You cannot withstand the storm.' The warrior whispers back, 'I am the storm.'
Meaning: Strength defies misfortune.
Origin: Unknown

46.What goes around, comes around
Meaning: Karma and destiny bring balance.
Origin: Proverb (English)

47. Don't count on luck—make your own
Meaning: Effort leads to success, not luck.
Origin: Unknown

48.Sometimes luck is just being prepared at the right time
Meaning: Preparation creates opportunity.
Origin: Unknown

49.Luck is not something you can mention in the presence of self-made men
Meaning: Hard work trumps luck.
Origin: E.B. White.

50.May luck and laughter light your days
Meaning: A common blessing for good fortune.
Origin: Irish Proverb.

End of Chapter 11

Chapter 12: Sayings About Honesty & Integrity

1.Honesty is the best policy
Meaning: Being truthful is always the right choice.
Origin: Benjamin Franklin.

2.What is right is not always popular, and what is popular is not always right
Meaning: Integrity means doing the right thing even when it's hard.
Origin: Albert Einstein.

3.A lie has short legs
Meaning: Lies are quickly exposed.
Origin: Proverb (Italian)

4.You can fool some people some of the time, but you can't fool all the people all the time
Meaning: Lies don't last forever.
Origin: Abraham Lincoln.

5.Tell the truth and shame the devil
Meaning: Being honest defeats deception.
Origin: William Shakespeare.

6.No legacy is so rich as honesty
Meaning: Honesty is one of the most valuable things you can leave behind.
Origin: William Shakespeare.

7.A clear conscience is a soft pillow
Meaning: Honest living leads to peace of mind.
Origin: German Proverb.

8.An honest answer is like a kiss on the lips
Meaning: Truthful words are valuable.
Origin: Biblical (reference)

9.If you tell the truth, you don't have to remember anything
Meaning: Honesty simplifies life.
Origin: Mark Twain.

10.Integrity is doing the right thing, even when no one is watching
Meaning: True character is shown in private actions.
Origin: C.S. Lewis.

11.Lies spread faster than the truth
Meaning: False information travels quickly.
Origin: Proverb (English)

12.A half-truth is a whole lie
Meaning: Omitting parts of the truth is still deception.
Origin: Yiddish Proverb.

13.Character is what you do when no one is watching
Meaning: Integrity means being honest at all times.
Origin: Unknown

14.A good name is better than riches
Meaning: Reputation is more valuable than wealth.
Origin: Dutch Proverb.

15.Deeds, not words, show honesty
Meaning: Actions reflect true integrity.
Origin: Proverb.

16. Better to be slapped with the truth than kissed with a lie
Meaning: Harsh truth is better than comforting deceit.
Origin: Russian Proverb.

17. When you stretch the truth, it snaps back
Meaning: Lies eventually lead to consequences.
Origin: Unknown

18. A liar should have a good memory
Meaning: Lies are hard to maintain.
Origin: Quintilian, Roman Rhetorician.

19. Truth fears no questions
Meaning: Honesty can withstand scrutiny.
Origin: Unknown

20. One lie leads to another
Meaning: Dishonesty creates a cycle of deception.
Origin: Proverb (English)

21. Trust is earned in drops and lost in buckets
Meaning: It takes time to build trust but only a moment to lose it.
Origin: Unknown

22. The truth may hurt for a little while, but a lie hurts forever
Meaning: Honesty is always the best long-term choice.
Origin: Unknown

23. Be truthful, or be silent
Meaning: If you can't tell the truth, it's better not to speak.
Origin: Arabian Proverb.

24. Trust takes years to build, seconds to break, and forever to repair

Meaning: Honesty is essential for maintaining relationships.
Origin: Unknown

25. Glass, china, and reputation are easily cracked and never well mended

Meaning: A damaged reputation is difficult to restore.
Origin: Benjamin Franklin.

26. A truth that's told with bad intent beats all the lies you can invent

Meaning: Truth can be misused just like lies.
Origin: William Blake.

27. One false move may lose the game

Meaning: A single act of dishonesty can have serious consequences.
Origin: Chess Proverb.

28. Truth is stranger than fiction

Meaning: Reality is often more unbelievable than made-up stories.
Origin: Mark Twain.

29. He who tells the truth must have one foot in the stirrup

Meaning: Speaking truth may lead to trouble.
Origin: Turkish Proverb.

30. Better to fail with honor than succeed by fraud

Meaning: Integrity is more important than winning dishonestly.
Origin: Sophocles.

31.Liars need good memories
Meaning: Keeping track of lies is difficult.
Origin: Unknown

32.An honest man's word is his bond
Meaning: A person of integrity keeps their promises.
Origin: Proverb (English)

33.Truth has no special time of its own. Its hour is now—always
Meaning: Truth is always relevant.
Origin: Albert Schweitzer.

34.A lie can travel halfway around the world while the truth is still putting on its shoes
Meaning: Falsehood spreads faster than truth.
Origin: Jonathan Swift.

35.You cannot serve two masters: truth and deceit
Meaning: One must choose honesty over lies.
Origin: Biblical (reference)

36.Honest people are the only ones worth trusting
Meaning: Integrity is the foundation of reliability.
Origin: Unknown

37.There is no wisdom like frankness
Meaning: Being direct and honest is the best policy.
Origin: Benjamin Disraeli.

38.False words are not only evil in themselves, but they infect the soul with evil
Meaning: Lies corrupt the individual and those around them.
Origin: Socrates.

39.The truth will set you free
Meaning: Honesty liberates you from guilt and deception.
Origin: Biblical (reference)

40.The biggest lie is the one you tell yourself
Meaning: Self-deception can be the most damaging.
Origin: Unknown

41.Speak the truth, even if your voice shakes
Meaning: Honesty takes courage.
Origin: Unknown

42.The reputation of a thousand years may be determined by the conduct of one hour
Meaning: Integrity can be lost in an instant.
Origin: Proverb (Japanese)

43.No man has a good enough memory to be a successful liar
Meaning: Lies are hard to maintain.
Origin: Abraham Lincoln.

44.Honesty is a very expensive gift. Don't expect it from cheap people
Meaning: Integrity is rare and valuable.
Origin: Warren Buffett.

45.Nothing is more honorable than a grateful heart
Meaning: Appreciation and honesty go hand in hand.
Origin: Seneca.

46.Integrity is telling myself the truth; honesty is telling the truth to other people

Meaning: Honesty begins with self-awareness.
Origin: Spencer Johnson.

47.People don't change, they reveal who they really are

Meaning: Over time, honesty exposes true character.
Origin: Unknown

48.Truth is the foundation of all virtue

Meaning: Honesty is at the core of good character.
Origin: Confucius.

49.The measure of a man's character is what he would do if he knew he would never be found out

Meaning: Integrity is acting rightly even in secret.
Origin: Thomas B. Macaulay.

50.Reputation is what others think of you; character is what you truly are

Meaning: Integrity matters more than public opinion.
Origin: John Wooden.

End of Chapter 12

Chapter 13: Sayings About Strength & Resilience

1. What doesn't kill you makes you stronger
Meaning: Challenges build resilience.
Origin: Friedrich Nietzsche.

2.Fall seven times, stand up eight
Meaning: Perseverance leads to success.
Origin: Proverb (Japanese)

3.A smooth sea never made a skilled sailor
Meaning: Difficulties build strength.
Origin: Franklin D. Roosevelt.

4.Strength does not come from physical capacity. It comes from **an indomitable will**
Meaning: True strength is mental, not just physical.
Origin: Mahatma Gandhi.

5.When the going gets tough, the tough get going
Meaning: Strong people push forward in adversity.
Origin: Joseph P. Kennedy.

6.Turn your wounds into wisdom
Meaning: Learn from hardships.
Origin: Oprah Winfrey.

7.A chain is only as strong as its weakest link
 Meaning; Team strength depends on individual resilience.
Origin: Proverb (English)

8. Tough times never last, but tough people do
Meaning: Resilient individuals outlast adversity
Origin: Robert H. Schuller

9.He who has a why to live can bear almost any how
Meaning: Purpose strengthens endurance.
Origin: Friedrich Nietzsche.

10.The bamboo that bends is stronger than the oak that resists
Meaning: Flexibility leads to resilience.
Origin: Proverb (Japanese)

11.Pain is inevitable. Suffering is optional
Meaning: Hardships happen, but your response is up to you.
Origin: Haruki Murakami.

12.Energy and persistence conquer all things
Meaning: Determination leads to success.
Origin: Benjamin Franklin.

13.The struggle you're in today is developing the strength you need for tomorrow
Meaning: Hardships build future strength.
Origin: Unknown

14.You may have to fight a battle more than once to win it
Meaning: Perseverance is key to overcoming obstacles.
Origin: Margaret Thatcher.

15. You never know how strong you are until being strong is your only choice

Meaning: Adversity reveals true strength.
Origin: Bob Marley.

16. Do not pray for an easy life; pray for the strength to endure a difficult one

Meaning: Resilience is more valuable than ease.
Origin: Bruce Lee.

17. It always seems impossible until it's done

Meaning: Even the toughest challenges can be overcome.
Origin: Nelson Mandela.

18. Build a strong foundation with the bricks others throw at you

Meaning: Use adversity as motivation.
Origin: David Brinkley.

19. Storms make trees take deeper roots

Meaning: Adversity strengthens character.
Origin: Dolly Parton.

20. Courage isn't having the strength to go on; it is going on when you don't have strength

Meaning: True strength is pushing forward in hardship.
Origin: Napoleon Bonaparte.

21. Sometimes you have to get knocked down lower than you have ever been to stand up taller than you ever were

Meaning: Hard times create stronger people.
Origin: Unknown

22. A river cuts through rock not because of its power, but because of its persistence

Meaning: Consistency leads to results.
Origin: James N. Watkins.

23. I am not what happened to me, I am what I choose to become

Meaning: Your response to adversity shapes you.
Origin: Carl Jung.

24. It is not the mountain we conquer but ourselves

Meaning: Overcoming challenges builds inner strength.
Origin: Edmund Hillary.

25. Hardships often prepare ordinary people for an extraordinary destiny

Meaning: Struggles build greatness.
Origin: C.S. Lewis.

26. Resilience is knowing that you are the only that has the power and responsibility to pick yourself up

Meaning: You Strength is your control.
Origin: Mary Hollow.

27. When life gives you lemons, make lemonade

Meaning: Find opportunity in adversity.
Origin: Elbert Hubbard.

28. When life gives you lemons, make lemonade.

Meaning: Find opportunity in adversity
Origin: Elbert Hubbard.

29. A hero is an ordinary individual who finds the strength to preserve and endure in spite of overwhelming obstacles
Meaning: True heroes are resilient.
Origin: Christopher Reeve.

30. Fire is the test of gold; adversity is the test of strong men
Meaning: Hardships reveal true strength.
Origin: Seneca.

31. Strength grows in the moments when you think you can't go on but keep going anyway
Meaning: Perseverance builds power.
Origin: Unknown

32. Tough times are like physical exercise—you may not like it while you're doing it, but tomorrow you'll be stronger because of it
Meaning: Difficulties build resilience.
Origin: Unknown

33. Only those who dare to fail greatly can ever achieve greatly
Meaning: Taking risks is part of growth.
Origin: Robert F. Kennedy.

34. Difficulties in life are intended to make us better, not bitter
Meaning: Challenges can lead to growth.
Origin: Dan Reeves.

35.Strength is not about how much you can handle before you break, but about how much you can handle after you break
Meaning: True resilience is bouncing back.
Origin: Unknown

36.What appears to be the end may actually be a new beginning
Meaning: Adversity often leads to new opportunities.
Origin: Unknown

37.Courage is not the absence of fear, but the judgment that something else is more important than fear
Meaning: Bravery is pushing forward despite fear.
Origin: Ambrose Redmoon.

38.Sometimes adversity is what you need to face in order to become successful
Meaning: Struggles are part of the journey.
Origin: Zig Ziglar.

39.Being challenged in life is inevitable, being defeated is optional
Meaning: You control how you respond to hardship.
Origin: Roger Crawford.

40. Strength is built by one's ability to keep moving forward despite obstacles
Meaning: Persistence leads to power
Origin: Unknown

41. Life's challenges are not supposed to paralyze you; they're supposed to help you discover who you are
Meaning: Adversity reveals character.
Origin: Bernice Johnson Reagon.

42. A diamond is a chunk of coal that did well under pressure
Meaning: Hardships refine people into greatness.
Origin: Henry Kissinger.

43. Every adversity, every failure, every heartache carries with it the seed of an equal or greater benefit
Meaning: Hardships lead to growth.
Origin: Napoleon Hill.

44. You can't cross the sea merely by standing and staring at the water
Meaning: Taking action builds resilience.
Origin: Rabindranath Tagore.

45. Life doesn't get easier, you just get stronger
Meaning: Challenges shape resilience.
Origin: Unknown

46. Fear does not stop death. It stops life
Meaning: Courage leads to full living.
Origin: Unknown

47. The oak fought the wind and was broken, the willow bent when it must and survived
Meaning: Adaptability is strength.
Origin: Robert Jordan.

48. Endurance is not just the ability to bear a hard thing but to turn it into glory
Meaning: Resilience turns hardship into success.
Origin: William Barclay.

49. A ship is always safe at shore, but that's not what it's built for
Meaning: Strength grows through challenges.
Origin: Albert Einstein.

50. Do not dwell in the past, do not dream of the future, concentrate the mind on the present moment
Meaning: Focus on resilience in the present.
Origin: Buddha.

Chapter 14: Sayings About Learning & Knowledge

1.Knowledge is power
Meaning: Understanding and information lead to influence.
 Origin: Francis Bacon.

2.The more you learn, the more you earn
Meaning: Education leads to success.
Origin: Warren Buffett.

3.Education is the passport to the future
Meaning: Knowledge prepares you for opportunities.
Origin: Malcolm X.

4.An investment in knowledge pays the best interest
Meaning: Learning provides long-term benefits.
Origin: Benjamin Franklin.

5.The only true wisdom is in knowing you know nothing
Meaning: Awareness of ignorance is the first step to knowledge.
Origin: Socrates.

6.A wise man can learn more from a foolish question than a fool can learn from a wise answer
Meaning: Learning depends on the listener, not the speaker.
Origin: Bruce Lee.

7. Tell me and I forget, teach me and I remember, involve me and I learn
Meaning: Active participation enhances learning.
Origin: Benjamin Franklin.

8. Live as if you were to die tomorrow. Learn as if you were to live forever
Meaning: Learning should be a lifelong pursuit.
Origin: Mahatma Gandhi.

9. The beautiful thing about learning is that no one can take it away from you
Meaning: Education is a lifelong asset.
Origin: B.B. King.

10. The mind is not a vessel to be filled, but a fire to be kindled
Meaning: Knowledge should inspire curiosity and growth.
Origin: Plutarch.

11. Wisdom begins in wonder
Meaning: Curiosity is the first step to gaining wisdom.
Origin: Socrates.

12. A journey of a thousand miles begins with a single step
Meaning: Great achievements start with small efforts.
Origin: Lao Tzu.

13. He who opens a school door, closes a prison
Meaning: Education reduces crime and hardship.
Origin: Victor Hugo.

14. Knowledge speaks, but wisdom listens
Meaning: True intelligence comes from understanding, not just speaking.
Origin: Jimi Hendrix

15. A person who never made a mistake never tried anything new
Meaning: Learning requires taking risks.
Origin: Albert Einstein.

16. Learning is a treasure that will follow its owner everywhere
Meaning: Education stays with you for life.
Origin: Chinese Proverb.

17. You don't understand anything until you learn it more than one way
Meaning: Mastery requires different perspectives.
Origin: Marvin Minsky.

18. The expert in anything was once a beginner
Meaning: All knowledge starts with inexperience.
Origin: Helen Hayes.

19. It does not matter how slowly you go as long as you do not stop
Meaning: Continuous learning leads to progress.
Origin: Confucius.

20. Wisdom is the reward you get for a lifetime of listening when you'd have preferred to talk
Meaning: Listening builds knowledge.
Origin: Doug Larson.

21. He who asks a question is a fool for five minutes; he who does not ask a question remains a fool forever

Meaning: Asking questions leads to learning.
Origin: Chinese Proverb.

22. The best way to predict the future is to create it

Meaning: Knowledge allows you to shape your destiny.
Origin: Peter Drucker.

23. Reading is to the mind what exercise is to the body

Meaning: Books nourish intelligence.
Origin: Joseph Addison.

24. Education is not the learning of facts, but the training of the mind to think

Meaning: Learning develops critical thinking.
Origin: Albert Einstein.

25. Knowledge without application is useless

Meaning: Understanding must be put to practical use.
Origin: Anton Chekhov.

26. A little knowledge is a dangerous thing

Meaning: Partial understanding can lead to mistakes.
Origin: Alexander Pope.

27. Ignorance is the night of the mind, but a night without moon and star

Meaning: A lack of knowledge leads to darkness.
Origin: Confucius.

28. Your mind is like a parachute—it only works when it's open

Meaning: Openness is key to learning.
Origin: Frank Zappa.

29. Learning never exhausts the mind

Meaning: Education keeps the brain active.
Origin: Leonardo da Vinci.

30. Teachers open the door, but you must enter by yourself

Meaning: Education requires personal effort.
Origin: Chinese Proverb.

31. Genius is 1% inspiration and 99% perspiration

Meaning: Hard work is key to mastery.
Origin: Thomas Edison.

32. A wise man never knows all; only fools know everything

Meaning: The intelligent recognize their limits.
Origin: African Proverb.

33. By seeking and blundering we learn

Meaning: Mistakes are part of education.
Origin: Johann Wolfgang von Goethe.

34. The capacity to learn is a gift; the ability to learn is a skill; the willingness to learn is a choice

Meaning: Learning is an active decision.
Origin: Brian Herbert.

35.Knowing yourself is the beginning of all wisdom
Meaning: Self-awareness leads to knowledge.
Origin: Aristotle.

36.Curiosity is the wick in the candle of learning
Meaning: Curiosity fuels the pursuit of knowledge.
Origin: William Arthur Ward

37.You can never be overdressed or over educated
Meaning: Knowledge and confidence are never excessive.
Origin: Oscar Wilde.

38.Not all readers are leaders, but all leaders are readers
Meaning: Reading cultivates leadership.
Origin: Harry S. Truman.

39.Education is the kindling of a flame, not the filling of a vessel
Meaning: Knowledge should inspire.
Origin: Socrates.

40.Knowing is not enough; we must apply. Willing is not enough; we must do
Meaning: Action is necessary for learning.
Origin: Johann Wolfgang von Goethe.

41.The only thing that interferes with my learning is my education
Meaning: Structured learning can sometimes limit curiosity.
Origin: Albert Einstein.

42. If you think education is expensive, try ignorance

Meaning: Lack of knowledge has a higher cost.
Origin: Derek Bok.

43. It is better to know how to learn than to know

Meaning: The skill of learning is more valuable than specific knowledge.
Origin: Dr. Seuss.

44. A candle loses nothing by lighting another candle

Meaning: Sharing knowledge benefits everyone.
Origin: James Keller.

45. Apply what you learn, and your learning will apply to you

Meaning: Practical application reinforces education.
Origin: Unknown

46. There is no wealth like knowledge, and no poverty like ignorance

Meaning: Education is the greatest resource.
Origin: Ali ibn Abi Talib.

47. Wisdom is not a product of schooling but of the lifelong attempt to acquire it

Meaning: Learning never ends.
Origin: Albert Einstein.

48.All knowledge is connected to all other knowledge.
The fun is in making the connections
Meaning: Everything learned contributes to a bigger understanding.
Origin: Arthur C. Aufderheide.

49.Mistakes are proof that you are trying
Meaning: Errors are part of the learning process.
Origin: Unknown

50.To know oneself is the beginning of wisdom
Meaning: Self-reflection leads to deeper understanding.
Origin: Socrates. \

End of Chapter 14

Chapter 15: Sayings About Courage & Strength

1.Courage is not the absence of fear, but the ability to act in spite of it
Meaning: Bravery means pushing forward despite fear.
Origin: Mark Twain.

2.Fortune favors the brave
Meaning: Those who take risks are more likely to succeed
Origin: Latin Proverb.

3.Do what you fear, and the fear will disappear
Meaning: Facing fears helps you overcome them.
Origin: David Joseph Schwartz.

4.Bravery is being the only one who knows you're afraid
Meaning: Courage isn't the absence of fear but persistence despite it.
Origin: Franklin P. Jones.

5.A hero is no braver than an ordinary man, but he is brave five minutes longer
Meaning: Perseverance defines courage.
Origin: Ralph Waldo Emerson.

6.It takes courage to grow up and become who you really are
Meaning: Self-discovery requires bravery.
Origin: E.E. Cummings.

7.Courage is resistance to fear, mastery of fear, not absence of fear

Meaning: Bravery means controlling fear, not avoiding it.
Origin: Mark Twain.

8.Success is not final, failure is not fatal: it is the courage to continue that counts

Meaning: Persistence defines success.
Origin: Winston Churchill.

9.Fear is only as deep as the mind allows

Meaning: Your thoughts determine the strength of your fears.
Origin: Proverb (Japanese)

10.He who is not courageous enough to take risks will accomplish nothing in life

Meaning: Success requires taking bold action.
Origin: Muhammad Ali.

11.A ship is safe in harbor, but that's not what ships are built for

Meaning: Comfort zones limit potential.
Origin: William G.T. Shedd.

12. Scared is what you're feeling. Brave is what you're doing

Meaning: Courage is action despite fear.
Origin: Emma Donoghue.

13.You cannot swim for new horizons until you have courage to lose sight of the shore

Meaning: Progress requires leaving comfort zones.
Origin: William Faulkner.

14.Courage doesn't always roar. Sometimes it's the quiet voice at the end of the day saying, 'I will try again tomorrow'
Meaning: Courage is persistence.
Origin: Mary Anne Radmacher.

15.It is not the strength of the body that counts, but the strength of the spirit
Meaning: Inner resilience matters more than physical power
. Origin: J.R.R. Tolkien.

16.Do the thing you think you cannot do
Meaning: Challenge yourself to overcome doubts.
Origin: Eleanor Roosevelt.

17.You gain strength, courage, and confidence by every experience in which you really stop to look fear in the face
Meaning: Overcoming fear builds courage.
Origin: Eleanor Roosevelt.

18.A brave man acknowledges the strength of others
Meaning: Courage means recognizing the value of others.
Origin: Veronica Roth.

19.Hardships often prepare ordinary people for an extraordinary destiny
Meaning: Struggles build character and strength.
Origin: C.S. Lewis.

20.If you are going through hell, keep going
Meaning: Perseverance leads to better times.
Origin: Winston Churchill.

.21.A warrior is not defined by how many battles he has won, but by the battles he has fought
Meaning: True courage is found in persistence.
Origin: Unknown

22.Be strong, you never know who you are inspiring
Meaning: Your courage influences others.
Origin: Unknown

23.Strength grows in the moments when you think you can't go on but keep going anyway
Meaning: Resilience is built through endurance.
Origin: Unknown

24.Sometimes courage is simply daring to take the first step
Meaning: Progress starts with action.
Origin: Unknown

25.Stand up for what is right, even if you stand alone
Meaning: Integrity requires bravery.
Origin: Unknown

26.The only thing we have to fear is fear itself
Meaning: Fear can hold you back more than real obstacles.
Origin: Franklin D. Roosevelt.

27.It's okay to be scared. Being scared means you're about to do something really brave
Meaning: Fear is part of courage.
Origin: Mandy Hale.

28.Bravery is the audacity to be unhindered by failures
Meaning: True courage means moving past mistakes.
Origin: Robert Greene.

29,Storms make trees take deeper roots
Meaning: Challenges strengthen individuals.
Origin: Dolly Parton.

30,The strongest people are not those who show strength in front of us but those who win battles we know nothing about
Meaning: Resilience is often unseen.
Origin: Unknown

31.Courage is found in unlikely places
Meaning: Bravery comes in many forms.
Origin: J.R.R. Tolkien.

32.Sometimes the smallest step in the right direction ends up being the biggest step of your life
Meaning: Small brave actions can lead to great changes.
Origin: Unknown

33.You never know how strong you are until being strong is the only choice you have
Meaning: Adversity reveals true strength.
Origin: Bob Marley.

34.Fear kills more dreams than failure ever will
Meaning: Avoiding challenges limits success.
Origin: Unknown

35.Strength is the product of struggle
Meaning: Difficulties build resilience.
Origin: Arnold Schwarzenegger.

36.Grit is not just simple elbow-grease term for rugged persistence. It is an often invisible display of endurance
Meaning: Strength is in persistence.
Origin: Sarah Lewis.

37.The only limits in life are the ones you make
Meaning: Courage is breaking self-imposed barriers.
Origin: Unknown

38.A river cuts through rock not because of its power, but because of its persistence
Meaning: Determination overcomes obstacles.
Origin: James N. Watkins.

39.Do not pray for an easy life, pray for the strength to endure a difficult one
Meaning: True strength comes from overcoming adversity
Origin: Bruce Lee.

40.Act as if what you do makes a difference. It does
Meaning: Every action, no matter how small, has impact.
Origin: William James.

41.The greatest test of courage is to bear defeat without losing heart
Meaning: Strength is in rising after failure.
Origin: Robert G. Ingersoll.

42.Fear has two meanings: Forget Everything And Run or Face Everything And Rise. The choice is yours
Meaning: Courage means choosing to face fears.
Origin: Zig Ziglar.

43.Endurance is not just the ability to bear a hard thing but to turn it into glory
Meaning: Courage transforms hardship into success.
Origin: William Barclay.

44.To live with courage is to live without limits
Meaning: Bravery expands opportunities.
Origin: Unknown

45.We don't develop courage by being happy every day. We develop it by surviving difficult times and challenging adversity
Meaning: Hardships shape resilience.
Origin: Barbara De Angelis.

46.No one saves us but ourselves. No one can and no one may. We ourselves must walk the path
Meaning: Courage is taking personal responsibility.
Origin: Buddha.

47.You cannot discover new oceans unless you have the courage to lose sight of the shore
Meaning: Adventure requires bravery.
Origin: André Gide.

48.Bravery is the capacity to perform properly even when scared to death
Meaning: Courage means taking action despite fear.
Origin: Omar N. Bradley.

49.Fear is temporary. Regret is forever
Meaning: Overcoming fear leads to long-term fulfillment.
Origin: Unknown

50.Life shrinks or expands in proportion to one's courage

Meaning: Bravery determines the possibilities in life.
Origin: Anaïs Nin.

End of Chapter 15

Chapter 16: Sayings About Love & Heartbreak

1. Love conquers all
Meaning: Love has the power to overcome any obstacle.
Origin: Virgil.

2. It is better to have loved and lost than never to have loved at all
Meaning: Experiencing love, even if it ends, is worthwhile.
Origin: Alfred Lord Tennyson.

3. The course of true love never did run smooth
Meaning: Love often involves difficulties.
Origin: William Shakespeare.

4. Absence makes the heart grow fonder
Meaning: Distance can strengthen love.
Origin: Thomas Haynes Bayly.

5. Love is blind
Meaning: Love doesn't always see flaws.
Origin: Geoffrey Chaucer.

6. Follow your heart
Meaning: Trust your emotions when making choices.
Origin: Unknown

7. You can't hurry love
Meaning: Love develops at its own pace.
Origin: Diana Ross.

8. Love is a battlefield
Meaning: Love can be full of struggles and challenges.
Origin: Pat Benatar.

9. Opposites attract
Meaning: People with different personalities can be drawn to each other.
Origin: Isaac Newton (adapted).

10. A broken heart hurts but it also teaches
Meaning: Heartbreak leads to personal growth.
Origin: Unknown

11. Love is like the wind, you can't see it but you can feel it
Meaning: Love is intangible but powerful.
Origin: Nicholas Sparks.

12. The greatest thing you'll ever learn is just to love and be loved in return
Meaning: Love is the most valuable experience in life.
Origin: Moulin Rouge.

13. Love makes the world go round
Meaning: Love is what keeps life meaningful.
Origin: W.S. Gilbert.

14. You never forget your first love
Meaning: The first experience of love leaves a lasting impact.
Origin: Unknown

15. Love is not finding someone to live with, it's finding someone you can't live without
Meaning: True love is essential to happiness.
Origin: Rafael Ortiz.

16. Where there is love, there is life
Meaning: Love gives life meaning.
Origin: Mahatma Gandhi.

17. Love is friendship set on fire
Meaning: Romantic love is deep friendship with passion.
Origin: Jeremy Taylor.

18. The heart wants what it wants
Meaning: Love is often irrational.
Origin: Emily Dickinson.

19. Love is like a flower, it needs time to bloom
Meaning: Love takes patience to grow.
Origin: Unknown

20. A life without love is like a tree without blossoms or fruit
Meaning: Love brings beauty and purpose to life.
Origin: Kahlil Gibran.

21. If you love someone, set them free. If they come back, they're yours; if they don't, they never were
Meaning: True love allows freedom.
Origin: Richard Bach.

22. Love is not about possession, it's about appreciation
Meaning: Love is based on valuing another person.
Origin: Osho.

23. To love and be loved is to feel the sun from both sides
Meaning: Love brings warmth and fulfillment.
Origin: David Viscott.

24. Love means never having to say you're sorry
Meaning: True love understands and forgives.
Origin: Erich Segal, *Love Story*.

25. You can't control who you fall in love with
Meaning: Love is unpredictable.
Origin: Unknown

26. True love stories never have endings
Meaning: Love is timeless.
Origin: Richard Bach.

27. Sometimes the heart sees what is invisible to the eye
Meaning: Love perceives things that logic cannot.
Origin: H. Jackson Brown, Jr.

28. Love isn't something you find. Love is something that finds you
Meaning: Love happens naturally.
Origin: Loretta Young.

29. Love and pain are two sides of the same coin
Meaning: Deep love often involves deep emotion.
Origin: Unknown

30. To love oneself is the beginning of a lifelong romance
Meaning: Self-love is essential.
Origin: Oscar Wilde.

31. Love is not about how many days, months, or years you have been together. It is all about how much you love each other every single day
Meaning: Love is measured by quality, not time.
Origin: Unknown

32. A heart that loves is always young
Meaning: Love keeps a person vibrant.
Origin: Greek Proverb.

33. A true love story never ends
Meaning: Real love lasts forever.
Origin: Unknown

34. Love is a journey, not a destination
Meaning: Love requires ongoing effort.
Origin: Unknown

35. There is no remedy for love but to love more
Meaning: Love is best cured with more love.
Origin: Henry David Thoreau.

36. We accept the love we think we deserve
Meaning: Self-worth affects our romantic choices.
Origin: Stephen Chbosky.

37. Love is composed of a single soul inhabiting two bodies
Meaning: True love is deeply connected.
Origin: Aristotle.

38. One love, one heart, let's get together and feel all right
Meaning: Love unites people.
Origin: Bob Marley.

39. Love doesn't make the world go round. Love is what makes the ride worthwhile
Meaning: Love gives life meaning.
Origin: Franklin P. Jones.

40. A soulmate is someone who makes you a better person
Meaning: True love helps you grow.
Origin: Unknown

41. The best proof of love is trust
Meaning: Trust is the foundation of love.
Origin: Joyce Brothers.

42. Love is the bridge between two hearts
Meaning: Love connects people.
Origin: Unknown

43. The best love is the kind that awakens the soul
Meaning: True love inspires personal growth.
Origin: Nicholas Sparks.

44. Love is like a puzzle. When you're in love, all the pieces fit, but when your heart gets broken, it takes a while to get everything back together
Meaning: Love requires patience and healing.
Origin: Unknown

45. You don't marry someone you can live with—you marry someone you can't live without
Meaning: True love is irreplaceable.
Origin: Unknown

46. Happiness is being married to your best friend
Meaning: Love is strongest when it's based on friendship.
Origin: Unknown

47. Love is a verb, not a noun
Meaning: Love is shown through actions.
Origin: Stephen R. Covey.

48. Love does not dominate; it cultivates
Meaning: Love helps people grow instead of controlling them.
Origin: Johann Wolfgang von Goethe.

49.The greatest happiness of life is the conviction that we are loved
Meaning: Love brings deep fulfillment.
Origin: Victor Hugo.

50.Love is a canvas furnished by nature and embroidered by imagination
Meaning: Love is shaped by emotions and creativity.
Origin: Voltaire.

End of Chapter 16

Chapter 17: Sayings About Food & Eating

1. You are what you eat
Meaning: Your diet affects your health and well-being.
Origin: Jean Anthelme Brillat-Savarin.

2. An apple a day keeps the doctor away
Meaning: Eating healthy foods promotes good health.
Origin: Proverb (English)

3. The proof is in the pudding
Meaning: The true value of something is shown through experience.
Origin: Proverb (English)

4. Don't cry over spilled milk
Meaning: Don't waste time worrying about things that can't be changed.
Origin: Proverb (English)

5. Too many cooks spoil the broth
Meaning: Too many people involved can ruin a task.
Origin: Proverb (English)

6. A watched pot never boils
Meaning: Time seems to move slower when you are waiting.
Origin: Benjamin Franklin.

7. Bite off more than you can chew
Meaning: Take on more responsibility than you can handle.
Origin: Proverb (English)

8. The best thing since sliced bread
Meaning: Something that is very useful or innovative.
Origin: Idiom (US)

9.Put all your eggs in one basket
Meaning: Don't risk everything on one opportunity.
Origin: Miguel de Cervantes.

10. You can't make an omelet without breaking a few eggs
Meaning: Progress often requires sacrifice.
 Origin: French Proverb.

11.Spill the beans
Meaning: Reveal a secret.
Origin: Slang

12.A piece of cake
Meaning: Something that is very easy to do.
Origin: Idiom (US)

13.Have your cake and eat it too
Meaning: Wanting everything without making sacrifices.
Origin: Proverb (English)

14.Full of beans
Meaning: Being energetic and lively.
Origin: Idiom (UK)

15.Take something with a grain of salt
Meaning: Be skeptical about something.
Origin: Latin Proverb.

16.Sell like hotcakes
Meaning: Something that is selling very fast.
Origin: Slang

17. Bring home the bacon
Meaning: Earn money to support oneself or a family.
Origin: Idiom (US)

18. Like two peas in a pod
Meaning: Very similar to each other.
Origin: Proverb (English)

19. Food for thought
Meaning: Something that makes you think deeply.
Origin: Idiom (English)
\

20. Cool as a cucumber
Meaning: Calm and composed.
Origin: Proverb (English)

21. Go bananas
Meaning: Act in a crazy or excited way.
Origin: Slang

22. A tough nut to crack
Meaning: A difficult problem or person.
Origin: Idiom (English)

23. Cherry on top
Meaning: Something extra that makes a good thing even better.
Origin: Slang

24. Butter someone up
Meaning: Flatter someone to gain favor.
Origin: Ancient Chinese Proverb.

25. Couch potato
Meaning: Someone who is lazy and watches too much TV.
Origin: Slang

26. Out of the frying pan into the fire
Meaning: Going from one bad situation to an even worse one.
Origin: Proverb (English)

27. Eat like a horse
Meaning: Eat a lot of food.
Origin: Idiom (English)

28. Eat humble pie
Meaning: Admit that you were wrong.
Origin: Proverb (English)

29. Egg on your face
Meaning: Feel embarrassed.
Origin: Slang

30. Forbidden fruit tastes the sweetest
Meaning: Things that are off-limits are the most tempting.
Origin: Biblical (reference)

31. One man's meat is another man's poison
Meaning: Something that one person likes may not be good for another.
Origin: Proverb (Roman)

32. Slow as molasses
Meaning: Very slow-moving.
Origin: Idiom (US)

33. It's the icing on the cake
Meaning: An additional benefit that makes something even better.
Origin: Idiom (English)

34. The breadwinner
Meaning: The person who earns the main income in a household.
Origin: Idiom (English)

35. To know which side one's bread is buttered on
Meaning: Understand what is in your best interest.
Origin: Proverb (English)

36. Cry over spilled milk
Meaning: Regret something that cannot be changed.
Origin: Proverb (English)

37. Eat your heart out
Meaning: Be jealous.
Origin: Idiom (US)

38. A bad egg
Meaning: A dishonest or unreliable person.
Origin: Proverb (English)

39. Eat to live, don't live to eat
Meaning: Focus on nutrition rather than indulgence.
Origin: Socrates.

40. Beggars can't be choosers
Meaning: People who rely on others can't be picky.
Origin: Proverb (English)

41. Gravy train
Meaning: An easy and profitable situation.
Origin: Slang

42. Have a lot on your plate
Meaning: Be very busy.
Origin: Idiom (English)

43. Tough cookie
Meaning: A strong and determined person.
Origin: Slang

44.Salt of the earth
Meaning: A very good and honest person.
Origin: Biblical (reference)

45.Burn the toast
Meaning: Mess something up or fail at cooking.
Origin: Slang

46.Sweeten the deal
Meaning: Add something extra to make an offer more attractive.
Origin: Idiom (English)

47.Bitter pill to swallow
Meaning: A difficult reality to accept.
Origin: Proverb (English)

48. If you can't take the heat, get out of the kitchen
Meaning: If you can't handle pressure, leave the situation.
Origin: Harry S. Truman.

49.A spoonful of sugar helps the medicine go down
Meaning: A little kindness makes tough situations easier.
Origin: Mary Poppins, *Disney*.

50.Bread is the staff of life
Meaning: Basic food sustains life.
 Origin: Proverb (English)

End of Chapter 17

Chapter 18: Sayings About Weather

1. Every cloud has a silver lining
Meaning: Even bad situations have positive aspects.
Origin: John Milton.

2. When it rains, it pours
Meaning: Problems often come all at once.
Origin: Proverb (English)

3. A storm in a teacup
Meaning: A big fuss over something unimportant.
Origin: Idiom (UK)

4. As right as rain
Meaning: Everything is perfect or going well.
Origin: Idiom (English)

5. Come rain or shine
Meaning: No matter what happens.
Origin: Proverb (English)

6. Chasing rainbows
Meaning: Pursuing something unattainable.
Origin: Idiom (English)

7. Make hay while the sun shines
Meaning: Take advantage of opportunities before they disappear.
Origin: Proverb (English)

8. Throw caution to the wind
Meaning: Act recklessly or without worry.
Origin: Idiom (English)

9.It never rains but it pours
Meaning: Troubles tend to come all at once.
Origin: Proverb (English)

10.Lightning never strikes twice in the same place
Meaning: Unlikely events don't happen in the same way twice.
Origin: Scientific Myth.

11.Snowed under
Meaning: Overwhelmed with work or responsibilities.
Origin: Idiom (UK)

12.Steal someone's thunder
Meaning: Take credit for another person's idea or success.
Origin: Proverb (English)

13.The calm before the storm
Meaning: A peaceful time before chaos.
Origin: Proverb (English)

14.Weather the storm
Meaning: Survive difficult times.
Origin: Proverb (English)

15.Cloud nine
Meaning: Feeling extremely happy.
Origin: Idiom (US)

16.Under the weather
Meaning: Feeling sick or unwell.
Origin: Proverb (English)

17.Break the ice
Meaning: Start a conversation in an awkward situation.
Origin: Idiom (English)

18.Bolt from the blue
Meaning: A sudden, unexpected event.
Origin: Proverb (English)

19.A breath of fresh air
Meaning: Something new and refreshing.
Origin: Proverb (English)

20.Stormy relationship
Meaning: A troubled and difficult relationship.
Origin: Idiom (English)

21.Head in the clouds
Meaning: Being unrealistic or distracted.
Origin: Idiom (English)

22.A fair-weather friend
Meaning: A friend who is only around in good times.
Origin: Proverb (English)

23.Cast a long shadow
Meaning: Have a strong influence over something.
Origin: Idiom (English)

24.Chilling to the bone
Meaning: Extremely cold weather.
Origin: Proverb (English)

25.Frozen in fear
Meaning: So scared you can't move.
Origin: Idiom (English)

26.A ray of sunshine
Meaning: Someone who brings happiness to others.
Origin: Proverb (English)

27.Hot under the collar
Meaning: Very angry.
Origin: Idiom (English)

28.Go with the wind
Meaning: Let things happen naturally.
Origin: Proverb (English)

29.A windfall
Meaning: An unexpected financial gain.
Origin: Proverb (English)

30.Cold hands, warm heart
Meaning: A kind person may not always show emotions outwardly.
Origin: Proverb (English)

31.The wind in your sails
Meaning: Encouragement or motivation to succeed.
Origin: Idiom (English)

32.A snowball effect
Meaning: A small action leading to bigger consequences.
Origin: Idiom (US)

33.Sow the wind and reap the whirlwind
Meaning: Actions have consequences.
Origin: Biblical (reference)

34.Spitting into the wind
Meaning: Wasting effort on something pointless.
Origin: Idiom (English)

35.To ride out the storm
Meaning: Endure a difficult situation until it passes.
Origin: Idiom (English)

36. A face like thunder
Meaning: A very angry expression.
Origin: Idiom (UK)

37. Red sky at night, sailor's delight. Red sky in the morning, sailors take warning
Meaning: A traditional weather prediction saying.
Origin: Nautical Proverb.

38. A blanket of snow
Meaning: A thick covering of snow.
Origin: Idiom (English)

39. Chilled to the bone
Meaning: Extremely cold.
Origin: Idiom (English)

40. Bright and breezy
Meaning: Cheerful and lively.
Origin: Idiom (English)

41. Dry spell
Meaning: A period without rain or without success.
Origin: Idiom (English)

42. A storm is brewing
Meaning: A difficult situation is developing.
Origin: Idiom (English)

43. Slick as ice
Meaning: Very slippery or smooth.
Origin: Idiom (English)

44. Lost in the fog
Meaning: Confused and uncertain.
Origin: Idiom (English)

45. A rolling fog
Meaning: Thick, moving fog.
Origin: Idiom (English)

46. High and dry
Meaning: Left in a difficult situation without help.
Origin: Proverb (English)

47. Sail close to the wind
Meaning: Take risks or push limits.
Origin: Idiom (UK)

48. Dead calm
Meaning: Completely still weather conditions.
Origin: Nautical Expression.

49. Cloud your judgment
Meaning: Make it difficult to think clearly.
Origin: Idiom (English)

50. Jack Frost nipping at your nose
Meaning: Very cold weather.
Origin: Idiom (US)

End of Chapter 18

Chapter 19: Sayings About Travel & Adventure

1. Not all those who wander are lost
Meaning: Exploration does not mean aimlessness.
Origin: J.R.R. Tolkien.

2. The world is a book, and those who do not travel read only one page
Meaning: Travel expands knowledge and experience.
Origin: Saint Augustine.

3. To travel is to live
Meaning: Travel enriches life.
Origin: Hans Christian Andersen.

4. Life is a journey, not a destination
Meaning: Enjoy the process, not just the goal.
Origin: Ralph Waldo Emerson.

5. A journey of a thousand miles begins with a single step
Meaning: Big adventures start with small actions.
Origin: Lao Tzu.

6. Travel broadens the mind
Meaning: Experiencing different cultures expands knowledge.
Origin: Proverb (English)

7. Take only memories, leave only footprints
Meaning: Respect nature and the places you visit.
Origin: Chief Seattle.

8. Adventure is worthwhile in itself
Meaning: The experience of adventure is valuable.
Origin: Amelia Earhart.

9. The road less traveled leads to the greatest rewards
Meaning: Choosing unique paths often brings the best experiences.
Origin: Robert Frost.

10. It's not the destination, but the journey that matters
Meaning: Enjoy the experience rather than just the end goal.
Origin: Unknown

11. Travel far enough to meet yourself
Meaning: Exploration leads to self-discovery.
Origin: David Mitchell.

12. Wanderlust: A strong desire to travel
Meaning: The urge to explore the world.
Origin: German Origin.

13. Travel is the only thing you buy that makes you richer
Meaning: Experiences are more valuable than possessions.
Origin: Unknown

14. A good traveler has no fixed plans and is not intent on arriving
Meaning: True travelers embrace spontaneity.
Origin: Lao Tzu.

15. The best journeys answer questions that in the beginning you didn't even think to ask
Meaning: Travel provides unexpected insights.
Origin: Jeff Johnson.

16. Go where you feel most alive
Meaning: Travel should be fulfilling and exciting.
Origin: Unknown

17. Wherever you go, go with all your heart
Meaning: Approach travel with enthusiasm.
Origin: Confucius.

18. Getting lost is not a waste of time
Meaning: Unexpected detours often lead to great discoveries.
Origin: Unknown

19. There are no foreign lands. It is the traveler only who is foreign
Meaning: Perception changes based on perspective.
Origin: Robert Louis Stevenson.

20. Collect moments, not things
Meaning: Experiences are more valuable than material goods.
Origin: Unknown

21. To awaken quite alone in a strange town is one of the most pleasant sensations in the world
Meaning: Travel provides excitement and freedom.
Origin: Freya Stark.

22. Traveling – it leaves you speechless, then turns you into a storyteller
Meaning: Experiences create great stories.
Origin: Ibn Battuta.

23. Half the fun of travel is the aesthetic of lostness
Meaning: Not having a plan can be part of the adventure.
Origin: Ray Bradbury.

24. Better to see something once than to hear about it a thousand times
Meaning: Experiencing something firsthand is more valuable than stories about it.
Origin: Asian Proverb.

25. Once a year, go someplace you've never been before
Meaning: Exploring new places is important.
Origin: Dalai Lama.

26. A ship in harbor is safe, but that is not what ships are built for
Meaning: Travel involves taking risks.
Origin: John A. Shedd.

27. Live your life by a compass, not a clock
Meaning: Let adventure, not schedules, guide you.
Origin: Stephen Covey.

28. The biggest adventure you can take is to live the life of your dreams
Meaning: Travel fuels ambition and discovery.
Origin: Oprah Winfrey.

29. Wherever you go becomes a part of you somehow
Meaning: Travel shapes your identity.
Origin: Anita Desai.

30. We travel not to escape life, but for life not to escape us
Meaning: Travel makes life more meaningful.
Origin: Unknown

31. Paris is always a good idea
Meaning: Some destinations are timeless.
Origin: Audrey Hepburn.

32. The journey is the reward
Meaning: Enjoy the experience, not just the goal.
Origin: Chinese Proverb.

33. Live with no excuses and travel with no regrets
Meaning: Embrace adventure without hesitation.
Origin: Oscar Wilde.

34. A traveler without observation is a bird without wings
Meaning: Learning from travel is essential.
Origin: Moslih Eddin Saadi.

35. Leave nothing but footprints, take nothing but pictures, kill nothing but time
Meaning: Be respectful while traveling.
Origin: Nature Conservation Saying.

36. Happiness is planning a trip to somewhere new
Meaning: The anticipation of travel brings joy.
Origin: Unknown

37. Travel is the healthiest addiction
Meaning: Exploring new places is rewarding.
Origin: Unknown

38. Adventure may hurt you, but monotony will kill you
Meaning: Routine can be stifling, while adventure brings excitement.
Origin: Unknown

39. People don't take trips, trips take people
Meaning: Travel has the power to transform.
Origin: John Steinbeck.

40. You don't have to be rich to travel well
Meaning: Good travel experiences don't require wealth.
Origin: Eugene Fodor.

41. There's no time to be bored in a world as beautiful as this
Meaning: Adventure is everywhere.
Origin: Unknown

42. I haven't been everywhere, but it's on my list
Meaning: The desire to travel is endless.
Origin: Susan Sontag.

43. Sometimes you have to travel a long way to find what is near
Meaning: Travel helps you appreciate home.
Origin: Unknown

44. One's destination is never a place, but a new way of seeing things
Meaning: Travel changes perspectives.
Origin: Henry Miller.

45. You can shake the sand from your shoes, but it will never leave your soul
Meaning: Travel stays with you.
Origin: Unknown

46. The impulse to travel is one of the hopeful symptoms of life

Meaning: Desire to explore keeps us moving forward.
Origin: Agnes Repplier.

47. Travel isn't always pretty. It isn't always comfortable. But that's okay. The journey changes you

Meaning: Travel transforms us.
Origin: Anthony Bourdain.

48. Some roads aren't meant to be traveled alone

Meaning: Some journeys are best shared.
Origin: Chinese Proverb.

49. Fill your life with experiences, not things. Have stories to tell, not stuff to show

Meaning: Memories are more valuable than possessions.
Origin: Unknown

50. A great way to learn about your country is to leave it

Meaning: Travel gives new perspectives on home.
Origin: Henry Rollins.

Chapter 20: Sayings About Animals

1. Let sleeping dogs lie
Meaning: Avoid stirring up trouble.
Origin: Proverb (English)

2. The early bird catches the worm
Meaning: Success comes to those who act early.
Origin: Proverb (English)

3. You can't teach an old dog new tricks
Meaning: It's difficult to change old habits.
Origin: Proverb (English)

4. Curiosity killed the cat
Meaning: Being too inquisitive can lead to trouble.
Origin: Proverb (English)

5. Every dog has its day
Meaning: Everyone gets a chance for success.
Origin: Proverb (English)

6. A leopard can't change its spots
Meaning: People don't easily change their nature.
Origin: Biblical (reference)

7. As sly as a fox
Meaning: Clever and cunning.
Origin: Idiom (English)

8. Birds of a feather flock together
Meaning: People with similar interests stick together.
Origin: Proverb (English)

9. Like a fish out of water
Meaning: Feeling uncomfortable in a new situation.
Origin: Idiom (English)

10. Don't count your chickens before they hatch
Meaning: Don't assume success before it happens.
Origin: Aesop's Fables.

11. Hold your horses
Meaning: Be patient and wait.
Origin: Idiom (US)

12. Make a mountain out of a molehill
Meaning: Exaggerate a small problem.
Origin: Proverb (English)

13. Straight from the horse's mouth
Meaning: Get information directly from the source.
Origin: Racing Terminology.

14. A little bird told me
Meaning: Heard information from a secret source.
Origin: Idiom (English)

15. There's more than one way to skin a cat
Meaning: There's more than one solution to a problem.
Origin: American Proverb.

16. When the cat's away, the mice will play
Meaning: People misbehave when not supervised.
Origin: Proverb (English)

17. Stubborn as a mule
Meaning: Extremely determined and unwilling to change.
Origin: Proverb (English)

18. Dog-eat-dog world
Meaning: A highly competitive and ruthless environment.
Origin: Idiom (US)

19. Kill two birds with one stone
Meaning: Achieve two things at once.
Origin: Proverb (Roman)

20. Crocodile tears
Meaning: Fake sadness or insincere emotions.
Origin: Ancient Greek Expression.

21. As busy as a bee
Meaning: Extremely active and hardworking.
Origin: Proverb (English)

22. Wolf in sheep's clothing
Meaning: Someone pretending to be harmless but is dangerous.
Origin: Biblical (reference)

23. Until the cows come home
Meaning: For a very long time.
Origin: Scottish Proverb.

24. A cat has nine lives
Meaning: Cats are resilient and often survive dangerous situations.
Origin: Proverb (English)

25. Like a bull in a china shop
Meaning: Very clumsy or reckless.
Origin: Idiom (English)

26. Mad as a hatter
Meaning: Completely crazy.
Origin: Lewis Carroll, *Alice in Wonderland*.

27.A fish rots from the head down
Meaning: Bad leadership affects everything.
Origin: Turkish Proverb.

28.Look what the cat dragged in
Meaning: Said when someone enters looking messy or unexpected.
Origin: Idiom (English)

29.An elephant never forgets
Meaning: Someone with a very good memory.
Origin: Idiom (English)

30. Like water off a duck's back
Meaning: Criticism or insults that don't affect someone.
Origin: Idiom (English)

31.A snake in the grass
Meaning: A sneaky and untrustworthy person.
Origin: Proverb (Roman)

32.Flogging a dead horse
Meaning: Wasting time on something that won't succeed.
Origin: Idiom (UK)

33.Barking up the wrong tree
Meaning: Looking in the wrong place for a solution.
Origin: American Proverb.

34.Raining cats and dogs
Meaning: Raining very heavily.
 Origin: Idiom (English)

35.Quiet as a mouse
Meaning: Extremely silent.
Origin: Proverb (English)

36. A wolf at the door
Meaning: Facing financial hardship.
Origin: Idiom (English)

37. To pig out
Meaning: To eat a lot of food.
Origin: Slang

38. A lame duck
Meaning: Someone or something that is weak and ineffective. Origin: Political Expression.

39. Happy as a clam
Meaning: Extremely content and happy.
Origin: Idiom (US)

40. As strong as an ox
Meaning: Very strong physically.
Origin: Idiom (English)

41. Eat like a bird
Meaning: To eat very little.
Origin: Proverb (English)

42. A one-trick pony
Meaning: A person who only has one skill or talent.
Origin: Idiom (US)

43. A pecking order
Meaning: A hierarchy or ranking system.
Origin: Animal Behavior Term.

44. Sitting duck
Meaning: An easy target.
Origin: Hunting Term.

45. As gentle as a lamb
Meaning: Very kind and harmless.
Origin: Idiom (English)

46. The straw that broke the camel's back
Meaning: A final problem that leads to failure.
Origin: Arabic Proverb.

47. Like shooting fish in a barrel
Meaning: Something extremely easy to do.
Origin: Idiom (US)

48. You can lead a horse to water, but you can't make it drink
Meaning: You can provide opportunities, but people must take them.
Origin: Proverb (English)

49. An eager beaver
Meaning: Someone who is very enthusiastic and hardworking.
Origin: Idiom (US)

50. A bird in the hand is worth two in the bush
Meaning: It's better to hold onto something certain than take a risk for more.
Origin: Proverb (English)

End of Chapter 20

Chapter 21: Sayings About Colors & Symbols

1. Once in a blue moon
Meaning: Something that happens very rarely.
Origin: Idiom (English)

2. Caught red-handed
Meaning: Caught in the act of doing something wrong.
Origin: Proverb (English)

3. Green with envy
Meaning: Feeling very jealous.
Origin: Shakespearean Origin.

4. Silver lining
Meaning: A positive aspect in a negative situation.
Origin: Idiom (English)

5. Golden opportunity
Meaning: A perfect chance.
Origin: Idiom (English)

6. Black sheep of the family
Meaning: A person who is different or considered a disgrace in their family.
Origin: Proverb (English)

7. White lie
Meaning: A harmless or small lie.
Origin: Idiom (English)

8. Paint the town red
Meaning: Go out and have a lively time.
Origin: Slang

9.Out of the blue
Meaning: Something unexpected.
Origin: Idiom (English)

10.Black and white
Meaning: Clear and obvious, with no gray area.
Origin: Idiom (English)

11.A red flag
Meaning: A warning sign of trouble.
Origin: Idiom (English)

12.Golden rule
Meaning: Treat others how you want to be treated.
Origin: Biblical (reference)

13.Blue blood
Meaning: A person of noble birth.
Origin: Spanish Origin.

14.Seeing red
Meaning: Feeling extreme anger.
Origin: Idiom (English)

15.Feeling blue
Meaning: Feeling sad or depressed.
Origin: Idiom (English)

16.Gray area
Meaning: Something that is unclear or undefined.
Origin: Legal Term.

17.In the black
Meaning: Financially profitable or successful.
Origin: Accounting Terminology.

18. In the red
Meaning: Losing money or in debt.
Origin: Accounting Terminology.

19. The grass is always greener on the other side
Meaning: People always want what they don't have.
Origin: Proverb (English)

20. Like gold dust
Meaning: Something rare and valuable.
Origin: Idiom (UK)

21. Tickled pink
Meaning: Very pleased or delighted.
Origin: Slang

22. Roll out the red carpet
Meaning: Give someone a grand welcome.
Origin: Hollywood Origin.

23. Purple prose
Meaning: Overly elaborate or flowery writing.
Origin: Literary Term.

24. Silver tongue
Meaning: A person who is persuasive or charming with words.
Origin: Idiom (English)

25. Greenhorn
Meaning: A newcomer or inexperienced person.
Origin: Slang

26. Golden handshake
Meaning: A large financial payment given to someone leaving a job.
Origin: Business Terminology.

27. A black mark
Meaning: A negative point against someone's reputation.
Origin: Idiom (English)

28. True colors
Meaning: A person's real character.
Origin: Idiom (English)

29. Born with a silver spoon in one's mouth
Meaning: Born into wealth and privilege.
Origin: Proverb (English)

30. White as a ghost
Meaning: Extremely pale, usually from fear.
Origin: Idiom (English)

31. In a brown study
Meaning: Lost in deep thought.
Origin: Idiom (UK)

32. As good as gold
Meaning: Well-behaved or valuable.
Origin: Idiom (English)

33. Black and blue
Meaning: Covered in bruises.
Origin: Idiom (English)

34. A golden touch
Meaning: An ability to be successful at everything.
Origin: King Midas Mythology.

35. Blue ribbon
Meaning: Sign of first place or excellence.
Origin: Idiom (US)

36. Like a red rag to a bull
Meaning: Something that provokes extreme anger.
Origin: Spanish Bullfighting Expression.

37. A silver bullet
Meaning: A simple solution to a complex problem.
Origin: Idiom (US)

38. A gray existence
Meaning: A dull or monotonous life.
Origin: Idiom (English)

39. A white-knuckle ride
Meaning: A very thrilling or scary experience.
Origin: Slang

40. Brownie points
Meaning: Gaining favor or approval.
Origin: Idiom (US)

41. Golden boy
Meaning: A young man destined for success.
Origin: Idiom (English)

42. Blue-collar worker
Meaning: A manual laborer or tradesperson.
Origin: American Business Terminology.

43. Red tape
Meaning: Excessive bureaucracy or official rules.
Origin: Government Terminology.

44. A black mood
Meaning: Feeling deeply unhappy or angry.
Origin: Idiom (English)

45. A silver lining in every cloud
Meaning: There is always some good in bad situations.
Origin: Proverb (English)

46. Paint yourself into a corner
Meaning: Create a difficult situation for yourself.
Origin: Idiom (English)

47. Yellow-bellied
Meaning: Cowardly.
Origin: Slang

48. Give someone the green light
Meaning: Give approval to proceed.
Origin: Traffic Signal Reference.

49. Like a deer in headlights
Meaning: Frozen in fear or surprise.
Origin: Idiom (US)

50. The silver screen
Meaning: The film industry or cinema.
Origin: Hollywood Expression.

End of Chapter 21

Chapter 22: Sayings About Numbers

1. Two heads are better than one
Meaning: Working together produces better results.
Origin: Proverb (English)

2. Third time's the charm
Meaning: Success comes after multiple attempts.
Origin: Idiom (English)

3. At sixes and sevens
Meaning: Being in a state of confusion or disorder.
Origin: Idiom (UK)

4. A stitch in time saves nine
Meaning: Fixing a problem early prevents bigger issues.
Origin: Proverb (English)

5. A dozen of one, half a dozen of the other
Meaning: Two choices that are essentially the same.
Origin: Idiom (English)

6. Seven-year itch
Meaning: Restlessness or dissatisfaction, often in marriage.
Origin: Idiom (US)

7. Two peas in a pod
Meaning: Two people who are very similar.
Origin: Proverb (English)

8. Five-finger discount
Meaning: Shoplifting or stealing.
Origin: Slang

9. Ten a penny
Meaning: Something very common or not valuable.
Origin: Idiom (UK)

10. Three's a crowd
Meaning: A third person is unwanted in a situation.
Origin: Idiom (English)

11. All in one piece
Meaning: Arriving safely without harm.
Origin: Idiom (English)

12. One for the road
Meaning: A final drink before leaving.
Origin: Slang

13. Four corners of the earth
Meaning: Everywhere in the world.
Origin: Biblical (reference)

14. Give someone a second chance
Meaning: Allow someone to try again.
Origin: Idiom (English)

15. A million and one
Meaning: A very large or exaggerated number.
Origin: Idiom (English)

16. On cloud nine
Meaning: Extremely happy.
Origin: Slang

17. Dressed to the nines
Meaning: Wearing very fashionable or elegant clothing.
Origin: Scottish Proverb.

18. At the eleventh hour
Meaning: At the last possible moment.
Origin: Biblical (reference)

19. One-track mind
Meaning: Obsessed with one thing.
Origin: Idiom (English)

20. Back to square one
Meaning: Starting over again.
Origin: Board Game Reference.

21. A hundred and ten percent
Meaning: Giving maximum effort.
Origin: Sports Terminology.

22. Two left feet
Meaning: Being clumsy while dancing.
Origin: Idiom (English)

23. Safety in numbers
Meaning: Being in a group reduces risk.
Origin: Proverb (English)

24. Behind the eight ball
Meaning: In a difficult or unlucky position.
Origin: Billiards Terminology.

25. Six feet under
Meaning: Dead and buried.
Origin: Idiom (English)

26. One step forward, two steps back
Meaning: Making progress but facing setbacks.
Origin: Idiom (English)

27. Zero in on something
Meaning: Focus closely on a target.
Origin: Military Terminology.

28. Luck of the draw
Meaning: Success or failure determined by chance.
Origin: Card Playing Terminology.

29. Knock seven bells out of someone
Meaning: To beat someone severely.
Origin: Idiom (UK)

30. A penny for your thoughts
Meaning: Asking someone what they are thinking.
Origin: Proverb (English)

31. Two's company, three's a crowd
Meaning: A third person can be unwanted in a group.
Origin: Proverb (English)

32. Third wheel
Meaning: Feeling unnecessary in a social situation.
Origin: Modern Expression.

33. Nine lives
Meaning: Surviving many difficult situations.
Origin: Reference to Cats.

34. Take five
Meaning: Take a short break.
Origin: Military Terminology.

35. Number cruncher
Meaning: Someone skilled with numbers.
Origin: Business Terminology.

36. All in due time
Meaning: Something will happen at the right moment.
Origin: Proverb (English)

37. Give an inch, take a mile
Meaning: If you allow a little, someone will take more.
Origin: Proverb (English)

38. Six of one, half a dozen of the other
Meaning: Two options that are equally good or bad.
Origin: Idiom (English)

39. A dime a dozen
Meaning: Very common and inexpensive.
Origin: Idiom (US)

40. Hundreds of times
Meaning: Repeated very frequently.
Origin: Idiom (English)

41. The whole nine yards
Meaning: Giving full effort.
Origin: Slang

42. Nine-to-five job
Meaning: A standard work schedule. Origin: Business Terminology.

43. First come, first served
Meaning: The first to arrive gets priority.
Origin: Proverb (English)

44. Three sheets to the wind
Meaning: Being very drunk.
Origin: Sailing Terminology.

45. A five-star experience
Meaning: An excellent and luxurious experience.
Origin: Hospitality Terminology.

46. Forty winks
Meaning: A short nap.
Origin: Idiom (English)

47. Two sides of the same coin
Meaning: Two things that seem different but are related.
Origin: Proverb (English)

48. Once bitten, twice shy
Meaning: Being cautious after a bad experience.
Origin: Proverb (English)

49. Ten out of ten
Meaning: A perfect score.
Origin: Grading Terminology.

50. One in a million
Meaning: Something very rare or unique.
Origin: Idiom (English) \

End of Chapter 22

Chapter 23: Sayings About War & Peace

1. War is hell
Meaning: War is brutal and destructive.
Origin: General William Tecumseh Sherman.

2. The best defense is a good offense
Meaning: Taking initiative is the best way to protect oneself. Origin: Military Strategy.

3. Divide and conquer
Meaning: Gaining power by splitting opposition into weaker groups.
Origin: Julius Caesar.

4. Know thy enemy
Meaning: Understanding your opponent is key to victory.
Origin: Sun Tzu, *The Art of War*.

5. Make love, not war
Meaning: Promote peace instead of conflict.
Origin: Anti-war slogan from the 1960s.

6. Loose lips sink ships
Meaning: Careless talk can lead to disaster.
Origin: World War II Propaganda.

7. Si vis pacem, para bellum
Meaning: If you want peace, prepare for war.
Origin: Latin Proverb.

8. An eye for an eye makes the whole world blind
Meaning: Revenge leads to endless conflict.
Origin: Mahatma Gandhi.

9. War does not determine who is right, only who is left

Meaning: War results in destruction rather than justice.
Origin: Bertrand Russell.

10. Old soldiers never die, they just fade away

Meaning: Veterans continue to exist beyond their service.
Origin: Douglas MacArthur.

11. Peace begins with a smile

Meaning: Kindness is the first step towards peace.
Origin: Mother Teresa.

12. He who wishes to fight must first count the cost

Meaning: War is costly and must be carefully considered.
 Origin: Sun Tzu.

13. The supreme art of war is to subdue the enemy without fighting

Meaning: Winning without conflict is the best strategy.
Origin: Sun Tzu.

14. In war, truth is the first casualty

Meaning: Deception and propaganda are common in war.
 Origin: Aeschylus.

15. Speak softly and carry a big stick

Meaning: Diplomacy backed by strength is effective.
Origin: Theodore Roosevelt.

16. One man's terrorist is another man's freedom fighter

Meaning: Perspective influences how people see conflict.
Origin: Unknown

17. War makes thieves, and peace hangs them

Meaning: War encourages crime that is punished in peacetime.
Origin: George Herbert.

18. War is a series of catastrophes that results in a victory
Meaning: Success in war often comes at great cost.
Origin: Georges Clemenceau.

19. Might makes right
Meaning: Strength determines justice.
Origin: Ancient Greek Philosophy.

20. You cannot shake hands with a clenched fist
Meaning: Peace requires openness and compromise.
Origin: Indira Gandhi.

21. Courage is resistance to fear, mastery of fear, not absence of fear
Meaning: Bravery means acting despite fear.
Origin: Mark Twain.

22. Better a bad peace than a good war
Meaning: Peace, even if imperfect, is better than war.
Origin: Russian Proverb.

23. Victory has a hundred fathers, but defeat is an orphan
Meaning: Success is widely claimed, while failure is abandoned.
Origin: John F. Kennedy.

24. No man is free who is not master of himself
Meaning: Self-discipline is essential for freedom.
Origin: Epictetus.

25. Those who live by the sword shall die by the sword
Meaning: Violence often leads to one's downfall.
Origin: Biblical (reference)

26. Only the dead have seen the end of war
Meaning: Conflict is a permanent part of human history.
Origin: Attributed to Plato.

27. If we don't end war, war will end us
Meaning: War threatens human survival.
Origin: H.G. Wells.

28. All war is deception
Meaning: Misinformation is a core strategy in war.
Origin: Sun Tzu.

29. We make war that we may live in peace
Meaning: Conflict is sometimes seen as necessary for stability.
Origin: Aristotle.

30. There never was a good war or a bad peace
Meaning: War is always harmful, and peace is always preferable.
Origin: Benjamin Franklin.

31. War is young men dying and old men talking
Meaning: Leaders wage war while soldiers suffer.
Origin: Unknown

32. A peace that comes from fear is not peace
Meaning: True peace must be built on justice, not intimidation.
Origin: Unknown

33. Freedom is never voluntarily given by the oppressor
Meaning: Liberty must be actively pursued.
Origin: Martin Luther King Jr.

34. Diplomacy is the art of letting someone else have your way
Meaning: Effective diplomacy manipulates without force.
Origin: Daniele Vare.

35. War is cruelty. You cannot refine it
Meaning: War is inherently brutal and cannot be made humane.
Origin: William Tecumseh Sherman.

36. To secure peace is to prepare for war
Meaning: Strength prevents conflict.
Origin: Ancient Military Strategy.

37. The pen is mightier than the sword
Meaning: Words have more power than violence.
Origin: Edward Bulwer-Lytton.

38. A just war is preferable to an unjust peace
Meaning: Not all peace is fair, and some wars are necessary. Origin: Cicero.

39. The enemy of my enemy is my friend
Meaning: Alliances are based on mutual opposition to a common enemy.
Origin: Ancient Proverb.

40. History is written by the victors
Meaning: Winners shape the narrative of events.
Origin: Winston Churchill.

41. No peace lies in the future which is not hidden in the present
Meaning: Future peace is shaped by current actions.
Origin: Unknown

42. A country cannot move forward by dwelling on war
Meaning: Nations must prioritize peace and growth.
Origin: Unknown

43. A war fought for power is never justified
Meaning: Motive determines the of conflict.
Origin: Unknown

44. More sweat in training, less blood in war
Meaning: Preparation reduces casualties.
Origin: Military Proverb.

45. Freedom isn't free
Meaning: Liberty requires sacrifice and defense.
Origin: American Proverb.

46. It is not enough to win a war; it is more important to organize the peace
Meaning: Post-war stability is as crucial as victory.
Origin: Aristotle.

47. War does not determine who is right – only who is left
Meaning: War results in destruction rather than moral victory. Origin: Bertrand Russell.

48. A truce is merely the seed of the next war
Meaning: Temporary peace often leads to future conflict
.Origin: Ancient Military Proverb.

49. Winning a war is easier than winning the peace
Meaning: Maintaining peace after war is a greater challenge.
Origin: Military Strategy.

50. War is the last refuge of the incompetent
Meaning: Only poor leadership resorts to war.
Origin: Isaac Asimov.

End of Chapter 23

Chapter 24: Sayings About Law & Justice

1.Justice is blind
Meaning: Fairness should be impartial and unbiased.
Origin: Legal Principle.

2.Ignorance of the law is no excuse
Meaning: Not knowing the law does not exempt one from following it.
 Origin: Legal Maxim.

3. A jury of one's peers
Meaning: A fair trial requires jurors from similar backgrounds.
Origin: English Legal System.

4.Beyond a reasonable doubt
Meaning: The highest standard of proof in criminal cases.
Origin: Legal Terminology.

5.Possession is nine-tenths of the law
Meaning: Ownership is often determined by who holds something.
Origin: English Common Law.

6.Let the punishment fit the crime
Meaning: Justice requires proportional consequences.
Origin: Gilbert & Sullivan, *The Mikado*.

7.A law unto oneself
Meaning: Someone who follows their own rules instead of society's.
 Origin: Idiom (English)

8.An eye for an eye, a tooth for a tooth
Meaning: Justice should be based on equal retaliation.
Origin: Biblical (reference)

9. A man is innocent until proven guilty
Meaning: The accused should be presumed innocent until convicted.
Origin: Legal Principle.

10. To err is human, to forgive divine
Meaning: Mistakes are natural, but forgiveness is virtuous.
Origin: Alexander Pope.

11. Truth will out
Meaning: The truth will eventually be revealed.
Origin: Shakespeare, *The Merchant of Venice*.

12. The wheels of justice turn slowly, but grind exceedingly fine
Meaning: Justice may take time, but it is thorough.
Origin: Ancient Proverb.

13. Speak the truth and shame the devil
Meaning: Honesty exposes wrongdoing.
Origin: Shakespeare, *Henry IV*.

14. The punishment must fit the crime
Meaning: Justice should be fair and proportionate.
Origin: Legal Doctrine.

15. A bad settlement is better than a good lawsuit
Meaning: Compromise is often better than legal battles.
Origin: Legal Wisdom.

16. He who represents himself has a fool for a client
Meaning: Legal self-representation is risky.
Origin: Legal Maxim.

17.No one is above the law
Meaning: Everyone is accountable under the law.
Origin: Legal Principle.

18.Hard cases make bad law
Meaning: Emotional cases can lead to poor legal precedents.
 Origin: Legal Maxim.

19.Better to let ten guilty men go free than imprison one innocent
Meaning: The justice system should err on the side of caution.
 Origin: William Blackstone.

20.A contract is a contract
Meaning: Legal agreements should be honored.
Origin: Legal Principle.

21.Guilty as sin
Meaning: Obviously guilty of wrongdoing.
Origin: Idiom (English)

22.A house divided against itself cannot stand
Meaning: Conflict weakens a group or society.
Origin: Biblical (reference)

23.Justice delayed is justice denied
Meaning: Delays in legal cases prevent real justice.
Origin: William E. Gladstone.

24.Throw the book at someone
Meaning: Give the maximum legal penalty.
Origin: Slang

25.No harm, no foul
Meaning: If no damage is done, no penalty should apply.
Origin: Legal Doctrine.

26. To take the law into one's own hands
Meaning: To seek justice without legal authority.
Origin: Legal Expression.

27. A fair trial
Meaning: Legal proceedings that ensure impartiality.
Origin: Legal Principle.

28. Liberty and justice for all
Meaning: A core ideal of fairness under the law.
Origin: American Pledge of Allegiance.

29. A witness to history
Meaning: Someone who has seen significant events.
Origin: Legal and Historical Expression.

30. A kangaroo court
Meaning: A biased and unfair trial.
Origin: Slang

31. Due process of law
Meaning: Fair legal proceedings must be followed.
Origin: Legal Principle.

32. A slap on the wrist
Meaning: A very light punishment.
Origin: Slang

33. A smoking gun
Meaning: Irrefutable evidence of wrongdoing.
Origin: Legal Expression.

34. The truth, the whole truth, and nothing but the truth
Meaning: An oath taken in court.
Origin: Legal Oath.

35.Habeas corpus
Meaning: The right to challenge unlawful imprisonment.
Origin: Legal Doctrine.

36.A matter of principle
Meaning: A legal or ethical stance that must be upheld.
Origin: Legal Concept.

37.Equal justice under law
Meaning: Everyone should receive fair treatment.
Origin: U.S. Supreme Court Motto.

38.Every man for himself
Meaning: People act in their own self-interest.
Origin: Legal and Social Concept.

39.A law-abiding citizen
Meaning: Someone who follows the law.
Origin: Legal Expression.

40.A case of mistaken identity
Meaning: Wrongly accusing someone.
Origin: Legal Term.

41.Dead to rights
Meaning: Caught in an undeniable crime.
Origin: Slang

42.A loophole in the law
Meaning: An unintended gap in legal rules.
Origin: Legal Terminology.

43.A necessary evil
Meaning: Something undesirable but required.
Origin: Legal and Ethical Concept.

44. Playing by the rules
Meaning: Acting within the law.
Origin: Legal Expression.

45. Above reproach
Meaning: Beyond any legal or moral criticism.
Origin: Legal Concept.

46. A breach of contract
Meaning: Breaking a legal agreement.
Origin: Legal Term.

47. A legal gray area
Meaning: A situation with unclear legal guidelines.
Origin: Legal Terminology.

48. Blind justice
Meaning: Justice that is impartial and fair.
Origin: Legal Symbolism.

49. To be held accountable
Meaning: To be legally responsible.
Origin: Legal Principle.

50. A legal loophole
Meaning: A technicality that allows someone to avoid a rule.
Origin: Legal Terminology.

End of Chapter 24

Chapter 25: Sayings About Sports & Competition

1.The ball is in your court
Meaning: It's your turn to take action.
Origin: Tennis Terminology.

2.No pain, no gain
Meaning: Hard work leads to success.
Origin: Fitness and Sports Culture.

3.Go the extra mile
Meaning: Put in extra effort to achieve success.
Origin: Sports and Motivation.

4.Hitting it out of the park
Meaning: Achieving great success.
Origin: Baseball Terminology.

5.Keep your eye on the ball
Meaning: Stay focused on your goal.
Origin: Baseball Terminology.

6.Play by the rules
Meaning: Follow fair and ethical practices.
Origin: Sports Ethics.

7.The home stretch
Meaning: The final phase of an endeavor.
Origin: Horse Racing Terminology.

8.A level playing field
Meaning: Fair competition for all participants.
Origin: Sports Terminology.

9. Throw in the towel
Meaning: Give up or surrender.
Origin: Boxing Terminology.

10. Sink or swim
Meaning: Succeed or fail on your own efforts.
Origin: Sports and Survival.

11. The underdog
Meaning: The competitor least expected to win.
Origin: Sports and Competition.

12. A race against time
Meaning: A competition to finish something before a deadline.
Origin: Sports Expression.

13. Second wind
Meaning: A burst of energy after exhaustion.
Origin: Running Terminology.

14. Step up to the plate
Meaning: Take responsibility and face a challenge.
Origin: Baseball Terminology.

15. On the ropes
Meaning: In a desperate or difficult situation.
Origin: Boxing Terminology.

16. Keep your head in the game
Meaning: Stay focused and alert.
Origin: Sports Motivation.

17. Hit the ground running
Meaning: Start something with enthusiasm and energy.
Origin: Running Terminology.

18. A marathon, not a sprint
Meaning: Long-term effort is required, not just short bursts.
Origin: Running Terminology.

19. Jump the gun
Meaning: Start too early, before being ready.
Origin: Track and Field Terminology.

20. Against the odds
Meaning: Succeeding despite difficulties.
Origin: Sports and Betting Terminology.

21. Drop the ball
Meaning: Make a mistake or fail to act.
Origin: American Football Terminology.

22. Out of left field
Meaning: Something unexpected.
Origin: Baseball Terminology.

23. Roll with the punches
Meaning: Adapt to difficult circumstances.
Origin: Boxing Terminology.

24. A game-changer
Meaning: Something that significantly alters the outcome.
Origin: Sports and Business Terminology.

25. Stay ahead of the curve
Meaning: Remain in a leading position.
Origin: Sports Strategy.

26. Pass the baton
Meaning: Hand over responsibility to someone else.
Origin: Relay Race Terminology.

27. Make a fast break
Meaning: Take advantage of an opportunity quickly.
Origin: Basketball Terminology.

28. Knocked out of the park
Meaning: Achieve great success.
Origin: Baseball Terminology.

29. The finish line is in sight
Meaning: The goal is almost achieved.
Origin: Running Terminology.

30. A slam dunk
Meaning: A guaranteed success.
Origin: Basketball Terminology.

31. Call the shots
Meaning: Make the important decisions.
Origin: Sports Coaching Terminology.

32. A fair-weather fan
Meaning: Someone who only supports a team when they are winning.
Origin: Sports Culture.

33. A winning streak
Meaning: A series of consecutive victories.
Origin: Sports Terminology.

34. Play your cards right
Meaning: Make the right decisions to succeed.
Origin: Sports and Gambling Terminology.

35. The thrill of victory and the agony of defeat
Meaning: The emotional highs and lows of competition.
Origin: Sports Broadcasting.

36.Foul play
Meaning: Unfair or dishonest behavior.
Origin: Sports Ethics.

37.Go for the gold
Meaning: Strive for the highest achievement.
Origin: Olympic Terminology.

38.Break a record
Meaning: Achieve an unprecedented accomplishment.
Origin: Sports Terminology.

39.A hat trick
Meaning: Three consecutive successes in a game.
Origin: Soccer and Hockey Terminology.

40.A home run
Meaning: A major achievement or success.
Origin: Baseball Terminology.

41.No holds barred
Meaning: No restrictions or limitations.
Origin: Wrestling Terminology.

42.A close call
Meaning: A situation that almost ended badly.
Origin: Sports and Racing Terminology.

43.Stay in your lane
Meaning: Focus on your own responsibilities.
Origin: Track and Field Terminology.

44.Caught off guard
Meaning: Taken by surprise.
Origin: Sports and Military Terminology.

174

45. A heavyweight
Meaning: A dominant or influential competitor.
Origin: Boxing Terminology.

46. A power play
Meaning: A strong strategic move.
Origin: Hockey and Business Terminology.

47. The crowd goes wild
Meaning: An excited response from spectators.
Origin: Sports Broadcasting.

48. A buzzer-beater
Meaning: A last-second winning score.
Origin: Basketball Terminology.

49. Skating on thin ice
Meaning: Taking a dangerous risk.
Origin: Ice Skating Terminology.

50. Down to the wire
Meaning: A competition that is decided at the last moment.
Origin: Horse Racing Terminology.

End of Chapter 25

Chapter 26: Sayings About Music & The Arts

1.Music is the universal language of mankind
Meaning: Music connects people across cultures.
Origin: Henry Wadsworth Longfellow.

2.Every artist was first an amateur
Meaning: Great artists start as beginners.
Origin: Ralph Waldo Emerson.

3.Art imitates life
Meaning: Art reflects real experiences and emotions.
Origin: Aristotle.

4.Strike the right chord
Meaning: Find the perfect balance or approach.
Origin: Musical Expression.

5.A picture is worth a thousand words
Meaning: Images can express meaning better than words.
Origin: Chinese Proverb.

6.The show must go on
Meaning: Performance must continue despite difficulties.
Origin: Theater and Music Expression.

7.March to the beat of your own drum
Meaning: Be independent and unique.
Origin: Musical Metaphor.

8.Break a leg
Meaning: A way to wish good luck in performing arts.
Origin: Theater Superstition.

9. Music soothes the savage beast
Meaning: Music has a calming effect.
Origin: William Congreve.

10. All that glitters is not gold
Meaning: Not everything that looks valuable is truly valuable.
Origin: Shakespeare, *The Merchant of Venice*.

11. A masterpiece takes time
Meaning: Great works of art require patience and effort
. Origin: Artistic Wisdom.

12. Lost in the music
Meaning: Completely absorbed in a musical experience.
Origin: Musical Expression.

13. Sing like no one is listening
Meaning: Express yourself freely without fear.
Origin: Inspirational Quote.

14. Dance to your own rhythm
Meaning: Live life according to your own unique style.
Origin: Dance Metaphor.

15. Pulling the strings
Meaning: Secretly controlling events behind the scenes.
Origin: Theater and Puppet Metaphor.

16. Play it by ear
Meaning: Adapt and respond as a situation unfolds.
Origin: Musical Terminology.

17. The pen is mightier than the sword
Meaning: Words and ideas are more powerful than violence.
Origin: Edward Bulwer-Lytton.

18. Paint with broad strokes
Meaning: Describe something in general terms.
Origin: Painting Metaphor.

19. Make a song and dance about it
Meaning: Exaggerate or overreact about a situation.
Origin: Idiom (UK)

20. The devil is in the details
Meaning: Small elements can make a big difference.
Origin: Design and Art Principle.

21. Encore!
Meaning: A request for an additional performance.
Origin: French for 'again' in theater and music.

22. Art is not what you see, but what you make others see
Meaning: Art is about evoking emotion and meaning.
Origin: Edgar Degas.

23. A picture paints a thousand words
Meaning: Visuals can communicate meaning more effectively than words.
Origin: Chinese Proverb.

24. Without music, life would be a mistake
Meaning: Music is essential to human experience.
Origin: Friedrich Nietzsche.

25. A virtuoso performance
Meaning: An exceptionally skilled artistic performance.
Origin: Musical and Artistic Terminology.

26. Fine-tune
Meaning: Make small adjustments to perfect something.
Origin: Musical Terminology.

27. A creative spark
Meaning: A moment of artistic inspiration.
Origin: Artistic Expression.

28. Hitting the high note
Meaning: Achieving a peak performance.
Origin: Music and Singing Metaphor.

29. Frame the discussion
Meaning: Shape the way a topic is presented.
Origin: Artistic Metaphor.

30. Paint yourself into a corner
Meaning: Create a difficult situation for yourself.
Origin: Painting Metaphor.

31. Stage fright
Meaning: Fear of performing in front of an audience.
Origin: Theater Terminology.

32. Pull out all the stops
Meaning: Go all out in an effort.
Origin: Organ Music Reference.

33. Sing from the same song sheet
Meaning: Work together with unity.
Origin: Musical Metaphor.

34. Take center stage
Meaning: Be the focus of attention.
Origin: Theater Expression.

35.Set the tone
Meaning: Establish the mood of a situation.
Origin: Musical Terminology.

36.A work in progress
Meaning: Something that is still developing.
Origin: Artistic Expression.

37.Jazz it up
Meaning: Make something more lively and exciting.
Origin: Jazz Music Influence.

38.Swan song
Meaning: A final performance or effort before retirement.
Origin: Mythology and Opera Reference.

39.Off-key
Meaning: Out of harmony, either in music or behavior.
Origin: Musical Terminology.

40.Drawing the line
Meaning: Setting boundaries.
Origin: Artistic and Painting Metaphor.

41.Hitting a sour note
Meaning: Doing something that causes a negative reaction.
Origin: Musical Expression.

42.A standing ovation
Meaning: Applause given by an audience standing up.
Origin: Theater and Music Recognition.

43.Steal the show
Meaning: To be the most impressive performer.
Origin: Theater and Performance Terminology.

44. Poetry in motion
Meaning: Something that moves with great beauty and grace. Origin: Poetic and Artistic Metaphor.

45. Choreograph your success
Meaning: Plan carefully for success.
Origin: Dance and Performance Metaphor.

46. A song in your heart
Meaning: Feeling happiness and inspiration.
Origin: Musical and Poetic Expression.

47. Dance like nobody's watching
Meaning: Live freely and without worry
Origin: Inspirational Quote.

48. Art for art's sake
Meaning: Art should be created for its own value, not for function
.Origin: Aesthetic Philosophy.

49. A blank canvas
Meaning: A fresh start or new opportunity.
Origin: Painting Metaphor.

50. Melody is the essence of music
Meaning: The tune is the most important part of a song.
Origin: Wolfgang Amadeus Mozart.

End of Chapter 26

Chapter 27: Sayings From the Bible & Religion

1.By the skin of your teeth
Meaning: Narrowly escaping a bad situation.
Origin: Biblical (reference)

2.A house divided cannot stand
Meaning: A divided group will fail.
Origin: Biblical (reference)

3.Do unto others as you would have them do unto you
Meaning: Treat others the way you want to be treated.
Origin: Biblical (reference)

4.Pride goes before a fall
Meaning: Arrogance leads to failure.
Origin: Biblical (reference)

5.A thorn in the flesh
Meaning: A persistent problem or burden.
Origin: Biblical (reference)

6.No rest for the wicked
Meaning: Evil people will always suffer consequences.
Origin: Biblical (reference)

7.Man does not live by bread alone
Meaning: Material things are not enough for life.
Origin: Biblical (reference)

8.An eye for an eye, a tooth for a tooth
Meaning: Punishment should be equal to the offense.
Origin: Biblical (reference)

9. The truth shall set you free
Meaning: Knowing the truth brings freedom.
Origin: Biblical (reference)

10. Let there be light
Meaning: A call for clarity and enlightenment.
Origin: Biblical (reference)

11. All things must pass
Meaning: Nothing lasts forever.
Origin: Biblical (reference)

12. Judge not, lest ye be judged
Meaning: Do not judge others harshly.
Origin: Biblical (reference)

13. Faith can move mountains
Meaning: Strong faith can overcome great challenges.
Origin: Biblical (reference)

14. The meek shall inherit the earth
Meaning: The humble will ultimately succeed.
Origin: Biblical (reference)

15. To everything there is a season
Meaning: Everything happens in its own time.
Origin: Biblical (reference)

16. Render unto Caesar what is Caesar's
Meaning: Separate religious and political matters.
Origin: Biblical (reference)

17.A prophet is not without honor except in his own country
Meaning: People often ignore wisdom from those they know.
Origin: Biblical (reference)

18.The writing on the wall
Meaning: A warning of inevitable disaster.
Origin: Biblical (reference)

19.Cast the first stone
Meaning: Do not judge unless you are without fault.
Origin: Biblical (reference)

20.Turn the other cheek
Meaning: Respond to wrongdoing with forgiveness.
Origin: Biblical (reference)

21.A good name is better than riches
Meaning: Reputation is more valuable than wealth.
Origin: Biblical (reference)

22.The powers that be
Meaning: Authorities in charge.
Origin: Biblical (reference)

23.Live by the sword, die by the sword
Meaning: Violence begets violence.
Origin: Biblical (reference)

24.As you sow, so shall you reap
Meaning: Actions have consequences.
Origin: Biblical (reference)

25.Salt of the earth
Meaning: A person of great worth and reliability.
Origin: Biblical (reference)

26.Many are called, but few are chosen
Meaning: Not everyone is selected for greatness.
Origin: Biblical (reference)

27.Straight and narrow
Meaning: A disciplined and moral path.
Origin: Biblical (reference)

28.The love of money is the root of all evil
Meaning: Greed causes many problems.
Origin: Biblical (reference)

29.Be fruitful and multiply
Meaning: Encouragement to grow and prosper.
Origin: Biblical (reference)

30.In the beginning was the Word
Meaning: A reference to divine creation.
Origin: Biblical (reference)

31.The Lord works in mysterious ways
Meaning: God's actions are beyond human understanding.
Origin: Unknown

32.Ashes to ashes, dust to dust
Meaning: Life is temporary.
Origin: Biblical (reference)

33.Where there is no vision, the people perish
Meaning: Leadership and guidance are essential.
Origin: Biblical (reference)

34.By their fruits you shall know them
Meaning: People's actions reveal their true character.
Origin: Biblical (reference)

35.To whom much is given, much is required
Meaning: Responsibility comes with privilege.
Origin: Biblical (reference)

36.The lamb shall lie down with the lion
Meaning: A vision of peace and harmony.
Origin: Biblical (reference)

37.Seek and ye shall find
Meaning: If you search, you will discover answers.
Origin: Biblical (reference)

38.Knock and the door shall be opened
Meaning: Persistence leads to opportunities.
Origin: Biblical (reference)

39.A city on a hill cannot be hidden
Meaning: Prominence brings visibility and responsibility.
Origin: Biblical (reference)

40.Man reaps what he sows
Meaning: One's actions determine their outcomes.
Origin: Biblical (reference)

41.Sufficient unto the day is the evil thereof
Meaning: Do not worry excessively about the future.
Origin: Biblical (reference)

42.The flesh is weak
Meaning: Human nature is prone to temptation
. Origin: Biblical (reference)

43.God helps those who help themselves
Meaning: Self-reliance is important.
Origin: Biblical (reference)

44.Faith without works is dead
Meaning: Actions must accompany beliefs.
Origin: Biblical (reference)

45.Let your light shine before others
Meaning: Be a good example.
Origin: Biblical (reference)

46.Suffer the little children to come unto me
Meaning: Children should be embraced and taught.
Origin: Biblical (reference)

47.The Lord is my shepherd
Meaning: God provides guidance and care.
Origin: Biblical (reference)

48.Vengeance is mine, sayeth the Lord
Meaning: Leave justice to God.
Origin: Biblical (reference)

49.The spirit is willing, but the flesh is weak
Meaning: People may have good intentions but lack strength.
Origin: Biblical (reference)

50.Let he who is without sin cast the first stone
Meaning: Do not judge others unless you are faultless.
Origin: Biblical (reference)

End of Chapter 27

Chapter 28: Sayings From Literature

1.To be, or not to be: that is the question
Meaning: The struggle of existence and choice.
Origin: William Shakespeare, *Hamlet*.

2.All that is gold does not glitter
Meaning: Not everything valuable is obvious.
Origin: J.R.R. Tolkien, *The Lord of the Rings*.

3.It was the best of times, it was the worst of times
Meaning: A contrast of great hope and despair.
Origin: Charles Dickens, *A Tale of Two Cities*.

4.Call me Ishmael
Meaning: A famous literary introduction.
Origin: Herman Melville, *Moby-Dick*.

5.Hell is other people
Meaning: Other people can make life unbearable.
Origin: Jean-Paul Sartre, *No Exit*.

6.I think, therefore I am
Meaning: Proof of existence through thought.
Origin: René Descartes, *Discourse on the Method*.

7.The pen is mightier than the sword
Meaning: Words and ideas have more power than violence.
Origin: Edward Bulwer-Lytton, *Richelieu*.

8.Something is rotten in the state of Denmark
Meaning: A sign of corruption and trouble.
Origin: William Shakespeare, *Hamlet*.

9. A rose by any other name would smell as sweet
Meaning: Names do not affect the nature of things.
Origin: William Shakespeare, *Romeo and Juliet*.

10. It is a truth universally acknowledged
Meaning: A famous opening line about societal expectations. Origin: Jane Austen, *Pride and Prejudice*.

11. All animals are equal, but some animals are more equal than others
Meaning: A critique of hypocrisy in power.
Origin: George Orwell, *Animal Farm*.

12. Big Brother is watching you
Meaning: A warning about government surveillance.
Origin: George Orwell, *1984*.

13. Beware the Ides of March
Meaning: A warning of impending doom.
Origin: William Shakespeare, *Julius Caesar*.

14. Do not go gentle into that good night
Meaning: A call to fight against death.
Origin: Dylan Thomas, *Poem*.

15. In my younger and more vulnerable years
Meaning: A reflective beginning to a novel.
Origin: F. Scott Fitzgerald, *The Great Gatsby*.

16. We are all fools in love
Meaning: Acknowledging the irrationality of love.
Origin: Jane Austen, *Pride and Prejudice*.

17. Tread softly because you tread on my dreams
Meaning: Respect the delicate dreams of others.
Origin: W.B. Yeats, *He Wishes for the Cloths of Heaven*.

18. You can't repeat the past
Meaning: A realization about the impossibility of reliving old times.
Origin: F. Scott Fitzgerald, *The Great Gatsby*.

19. Not all those who wander are lost
Meaning: Exploring life does not mean being aimless.
Origin: J.R.R. Tolkien, *The Lord of the Rings*.

20. Et tu, Brute?
Meaning: A phrase of ultimate betrayal.
Origin: William Shakespeare, *Julius Caesar*.

21. There is no greater agony than bearing an untold story inside you
Meaning: The pain of unexpressed emotions.
Origin: Maya Angelou, *I Know Why the Caged Bird Sings*.

22. Parting is such sweet sorrow
Meaning: Goodbye is bittersweet.
Origin: William Shakespeare, *Romeo and Juliet*.

23. So we beat on, boats against the current
Meaning: A reflection on the struggle of moving forward.
Origin: F. Scott Fitzgerald, *The Great Gatsby*.

24. A thing of beauty is a joy forever
Meaning: True beauty has lasting value.
Origin: John Keats, *Endymion*.

25. War is peace. Freedom is slavery. Ignorance is strength.
Meaning: A paradox of authoritarian rule.
Origin: George Orwell, *1984*.

26. We are such stuff as dreams are made on
Meaning: Life is fleeting and dreamlike.
Origin: William Shakespeare, *The Tempest*.

27. Elementary, my dear Watson
Meaning: A catchphrase for deductive reasoning.
Origin: Sir Arthur Conan Doyle (paraphrased).

28. The world breaks everyone
Meaning: Hardship is universal.
Origin: Ernest Hemingway, *A Farewell to Arms*.

29. To love or have loved, that is enough
Meaning: Love is the ultimate experience.
Origin: Victor Hugo, *Les Misérables*.

30. All we have to decide is what to do with the time that is given us
Meaning: Life is about choices.
Origin: J.R.R. Tolkien, *The Lord of the Rings*.

31. After all, tomorrow is another day
Meaning: A hopeful look at the future.
Origin: Margaret Mitchell, *Gone with the Wind*.

32. There is no place like home
Meaning: Home is the most comforting place.
Origin: L. Frank Baum, *The Wizard of Oz*.

33. Fear leads to anger, anger leads to hate, hate leads to suffering
Meaning: A warning against negative emotions.
Origin: George Lucas, *Star Wars*.

34.It matters not what someone is born, but what they grow to be
Meaning: Character is shaped by choices.
Origin: J.K. Rowling, *Harry Potter*.

35.I wish you to know that you have been the last dream of my soul
Meaning: A deeply emotional farewell.
Origin: Charles Dickens, *A Tale of Two Cities*.

36.Rage, rage against the dying of the light
Meaning: A passionate refusal to accept death.
Origin: Dylan Thomas, *Poem*.

37.I have loved the stars too fondly to be fearful of the night
Meaning: Finding comfort in the unknown.
Origin: Sarah Williams, *The Old Astronomer*.

38.Whatever our souls are made of, his and mine are the same
Meaning: A deep connection between two people.
Origin: Emily Brontë, *Wuthering Heights*.

39.Fairy tales are more than true
Meaning: Stories shape our understanding of the world.
Origin: Neil Gaiman, *Coraline*.

40. That's one small step for man, one giant leap for mankind
Meaning: A historic moment of progress.
Origin: Neil Armstrong (Quoted in History).

41. Of all the gin joints in all the towns in all the world, she walks into mine
Meaning: A lament about fate.
Origin: Casablanca (Movie Adaptation).

42. We accept the love we think we deserve
Meaning: Self-worth affects relationships.
Origin: Stephen Chbosky, *The Perks of Being a Wallflower*.

43. Life is to be lived, not controlled
Meaning: Emphasizing the importance of free will.
Origin: Ralph Ellison, *Invisible Man*.

44. Beware; for I am fearless, and therefore powerful
Meaning: Fearlessness brings great strength.
Origin: Mary Shelley, *Frankenstein*.

45. It does not do to dwell on dreams and forget to live
Meaning: Balance ambition with reality.
Origin: J.K. Rowling, *Harry Potter*.

46. Happiness can be found even in the darkest of times
Meaning: Hope persists through struggles.
Origin: J.K. Rowling, *Harry Potter*.

47. He who opens a school door, closes a prison
Meaning: Education is the key to freedom.
Origin: Unknown

48. Not all those who wander are lost
Meaning: Exploring life does not mean being aimless.
Origin: J.R.R. Tolkien, *The Lord of the Rings*.

49. When you play the game of thrones, you win or you die
Meaning: There is no middle ground in power struggles.
Origin: George R.R. Martin, *Game of Thrones*.

50. People generally see what they look for, and hear what they listen for
Meaning: Perception shapes reality.
Origin: Harper Lee, *To Kill a Mockingbird*.

End of Chapter 28

Chapter 29: Sayings From Ancient Cultures

1. Know thyself
Meaning: Understanding yourself is the key to wisdom.
Origin: Ancient Greek, Temple of Apollo at Delphi.

2. Fortune favors the bold
Meaning: Taking risks leads to success.
Origin: Latin Proverb, Virgil.

3. When in Rome, do as the Romans do
Meaning: Adapt to local customs.
Origin: Proverb (Roman)

4. An eye for an eye leaves the whole world blind
Meaning: Revenge is ultimately destructive.
Origin: Ancient Indian Wisdom, Gandhi.

5. The journey of a thousand miles begins with a single step
Meaning: Great things start with small beginnings.
Origin: Lao Tzu, Ancient China.

6. Beware of Greeks bearing gifts
Meaning: Be cautious of hidden motives.
Origin: Ancient Greek, The Trojan War Myth.

7. A fool and his money are soon parted
Meaning: Careless people lose their wealth.
Origin: Proverb (English)

8. The nail that sticks out gets hammered down
Meaning: Conformity is often enforced.
Origin: Proverb (Japanese)

9. He who opens a school door, closes a prison
Meaning: Education leads to freedom.
Origin: Ancient Chinese Proverb.

10. The wise man learns more from his enemies than a fool from his friends
Meaning: Adversity can be a great teacher.
Origin: Ancient Greek Proverb.

11. To run with the hare and hunt with the hounds
Meaning: Trying to stay on both sides of a conflict.
Origin: Proverb (English)

12. It is better to be a warrior in a garden than a gardener in a war
Meaning: Be prepared for difficulties even in peace.
Origin: Ancient Samurai Wisdom.

13. A man is known by the company he keeps
Meaning: Your character is judged by your associations.
Origin: Ancient Greek Wisdom, Aesop.

14. Do not count your chickens before they hatch
Meaning: Do not assume success before it happens.
Origin: Aesop's Fables, Ancient Greece.

15. Build your house on solid rock
Meaning: A strong foundation leads to stability.
Origin: Biblical (reference)

16. Even a broken clock is right twice a day
Meaning: Mistakes or flawed things can still be correct occasionally
.Origin: Ancient Chinese Proverb.

17. If you chase two rabbits, you will catch neither
Meaning: Focus on one goal at a time.
Origin: Ancient Russian Proverb.

18. An army marches on its stomach
Meaning: Logistics and food are essential for success.
Origin: Napoleon Bonaparte, Ancient War Strategy.

19. A lion does not concern itself with the opinion of sheep
Meaning: Strong leaders do not worry about weak critics.
 Origin: Ancient African Proverb.

20. If you want to go fast, go alone. If you want to go far, go together
Meaning: Collaboration leads to greater achievements.
Origin: Ancient African Wisdom.

21. The enemy of my enemy is my friend
Meaning: Common opposition can create alliances.
Origin: Ancient Indian and Arabic Proverb.

22. Walls have ears
Meaning: Be careful what you say, as someone may be listening
. Origin: Ancient Egyptian Proverb.

23. Death is lighter than a feather, duty heavier than a mountain
Meaning: Honor outweighs personal comfort.
Origin: Proverb (Japanese)

24. Opportunity knocks but once
Meaning: Do not miss rare opportunities.
Origin: Ancient Roman Wisdom.

25. A journey well begun is half done
Meaning: Starting well is crucial to success.
Origin: Ancient Greek Wisdom.

26. One does not sharpen the axe after arriving in the battlefield
Meaning: Prepare before facing a challenge.
Origin: Ancient Indian Proverb.

27. An inch of time is worth an inch of gold
Meaning: Time is valuable.
Origin: Ancient Chinese Proverb.

28. There are no shortcuts to the top of the palm tree
Meaning: Success requires effort.
Origin: Ancient African Proverb.

29. The gods help those who help themselves
Meaning: Self-reliance leads to divine favor.
Origin: Ancient Greek Proverb.

30. The more you know, the less you need
Meaning: Wisdom simplifies life.
Origin: Ancient Aboriginal Proverb.

31. The weak can never forgive. Forgiveness is the attribute of the strong
Meaning: Forgiving requires strength.
Origin: Ancient Indian Wisdom, Mahatma Gandhi.

32. The greatest wealth is to live content with little
Meaning: Simplicity brings happiness.
Origin: Plato, Ancient Greece.

33. He who asks is a fool for five minutes, but he who does not ask remains a fool forever
Meaning: Asking questions leads to wisdom.
Origin: Ancient Chinese Proverb.

34. A wise man adapts himself to circumstances
Meaning: Flexibility is key to survival.
Origin: Ancient Roman Wisdom.

35. The hunter who chases two rabbits will catch neither
Meaning: Pursuing too many goals leads to failure.
Origin: Ancient Chinese Proverb.

36. Don't put all your eggs in one basket
Meaning: Diversify to reduce risk.
Origin: Ancient Spanish Proverb.

37. Words should be weighed, not counted
Meaning: Quality matters more than quantity.
Origin: Ancient Yiddish Proverb.

38. Where there is no vision, the people perish
Meaning: Leadership requires foresight.
Origin: Biblical (reference)

39. The man who removes a mountain begins by carrying away small stones
Meaning: Big challenges require small steps.
Origin: Ancient Chinese Proverb.

40. Water will wear away stone
Meaning: Persistence leads to results.
Origin: Ancient Eastern Wisdom.

41. If there is no enemy within, the enemy outside can do you no harm
Meaning: Self-discipline prevents external failures.
Origin: African Proverb.

42. A man who stands on tiptoe is not steady
Meaning: Overconfidence can lead to instability.
Origin: Lao Tzu, Ancient China.

43. A society grows great when old men plant trees whose shade they know they shall never sit in
Meaning: Building a better future benefits later generations.
 Origin: Ancient Greek Proverb.

44. One moment of patience may ward off disaster
Meaning: Patience prevents mistakes.
Origin: Ancient Chinese Proverb.

45. The wise man does not lay up treasure, but only what he needs
Meaning: Excessive greed is unnecessary.
Origin: Lao Tzu, Ancient China.

46. A candle loses nothing by lighting another candle
Meaning: Helping others does not diminish oneself.
Origin: Ancient Buddhist Wisdom.

47. The river is formed drop by drop
Meaning: Small efforts accumulate over time.
Origin: Ancient Persian Proverb.

48. Wisdom begins in wonder
Meaning: Curiosity leads to knowledge.
Origin: Socrates, Ancient Greece.

49.A fool speaks, a wise man listens
Meaning: Listening is more valuable than speaking.
Origin: Ancient Egyptian Proverb.

50.Dig the well before you are thirsty
Meaning: Prepare for future needs.
Origin: Ancient Chinese Proverb

End of Chapter 29

Chapter 30: Sayings From Different Countries

1. The squeaky wheel gets the grease
Meaning: Those who speak up receive attention.
Origin: American Proverb.

2. Measure seven times, cut once
Meaning: Think carefully before acting.
Origin: Russian Proverb.

3. Where there's a will, there's a way
Meaning: Determination leads to success.
Origin: Proverb (English)

4. A leopard cannot change its spots
Meaning: People do not change their true nature.
Origin: African Proverb.

5. The enemy of my enemy is my friend
Meaning: Common adversaries can create alliances.
Origin: Arabic Proverb.

6. Even monkeys fall from trees
Meaning: Everyone makes mistakes
Origin: Proverb (Japanese)

7. He who has health has hope, and he who has hope has
everything
Meaning: Good health is key to happiness.
Origin: Arab Proverb.

8. A closed mouth catches no flies
Meaning: Staying silent can prevent trouble.
Origin: French Proverb.

9. Do not wake a sleeping dog
Meaning: Avoid unnecessary trouble.
Origin: German Proverb.

10. A bird in the hand is worth two in the bush
Meaning: A guaranteed benefit is better than a possible one.
Origin: Proverb (English)

11. A hungry belly has no ears
Meaning: People cannot focus when hungry.
Origin: Greek Proverb.

12. Drop by drop, the bucket gets filled
Meaning: Small efforts lead to big results.
Origin: Proverb (Italian)

13. The fish rots from the head down
Meaning: Leadership problems affect the whole group.
Origin: Turkish Proverb.

14. A cat in gloves catches no mice
Meaning: Over-caution prevents success.
Origin: Spanish Proverb.

15. Do not sell the skin before you catch the bear
Meaning: Do not celebrate before securing success.
Origin: Finnish Proverb.

16. If you want to go fast, go alone; if you want to go far, go together
Meaning: Teamwork leads to lasting success.
Origin: African Proverb.

17.It is not the horse that draws the cart, but the oats
Meaning: Motivation drives success.
Origin: Russian Proverb.

18.Better to be a free dog than a caged lion
Meaning: Freedom is more valuable than status.
Origin: Chinese Proverb.

19.Even a clock that does not work is right twice a day
Meaning: Flawed things can still be correct sometimes.
Origin: Polish Proverb.

20.Do not count your chickens before they hatch
Meaning: Do not assume success too soon.
Origin: Portuguese Proverb.

21. You can't have your cake and eat it too
Meaning: You cannot enjoy both extremes at the same time.
Origin: Proverb (English)

22.When the wind blows, some build walls, others build windmills
Meaning: Challenges can be turned into opportunities.
Origin: Chinese Proverb.

23.An old friend is better than two new ones
Meaning: Loyalty is valuable.
Origin: Georgian Proverb

24.Do not put out the fire while your house is still burning
Meaning: Solve the real problem before celebrating.
Origin: Russian Proverb.

25. You reap what you sow
Meaning: Your actions determine your outcomes.
Origin: Biblical (reference)

26. A guest sees more in an hour than a host sees in a year
Meaning: Outsiders notice things that locals overlook.
Origin: Polish Proverb.

27. You cannot clap with one hand
Meaning: Success requires teamwork.
Origin: Indian Proverb.

28. A single bracelet does not jingle
Meaning: Collaboration leads to success.
Origin: African Proverb.

29. To learn a language is to have one more window to look at the world
Meaning: Knowledge expands perspective.
Origin: Chinese Proverb.

30. Rats leave a sinking ship
Meaning: People abandon failing causes.
Origin: French Proverb.

31. A donkey always finds a way into a roofless house
Meaning: Opportunists exploit weak situations.
Origin: Turkish Proverb.

32.If you chase two rabbits, you will catch neither
Meaning: Focus on one goal at a time.
Origin: Russian Proverb.

33.A single spark can start a prairie fire
Meaning: Small actions can lead to great changes.
Origin: Chinese Proverb.

34.One hand washes the other
Meaning: Mutual assistance benefits both parties.
Origin: Proverb (Italian)

35.A fool and his money are soon parted
Meaning: Careless people lose their wealth.
Origin: Proverb (English)

36.The nail that sticks out gets hammered down
Meaning: Conformity is often enforced.
Origin: Proverb (Japanese)

37.Give a man a fish, and he will eat for a day; teach a man to fish, and he will eat for a lifetime
Meaning: Skills are more valuable than temporary help.
Origin: Chinese Proverb.

38.There is no shame in not knowing, but shame in not learning
Meaning: Ignorance is acceptable, but unwillingness to learn is not.
Origin: Russian Proverb.

39.No matter how far you have gone down the wrong road, turn back
Meaning: It is never too late to correct mistakes.
Origin: Turkish Proverb.

40. All roads lead to Rome
Meaning: Different paths can lead to the same goal.
Origin: Latin Proverb.

41. Talk does not cook rice
Meaning: Action is needed, not just words.
Origin: Chinese Proverb.

42. God gives nuts to those who have no teeth
Meaning: Opportunities are often wasted on those who cannot use them.
Origin: Spanish Proverb.

43. The darkest hour is just before the dawn
Meaning: Hope follows hardship.
Origin: Proverb (English)

44. A drowning man will clutch at a straw
Meaning: Desperate people try anything.
Origin: Dutch Proverb.

45. To understand all is to forgive all
Meaning: Understanding leads to empathy.
Origin: French Proverb.

46. A bad workman blames his tools
Meaning: People blame external factors for their own failures.
Origin: Proverb (English)

47. A rolling stone gathers no moss
Meaning: Constant movement prevents stability.
Origin: Latin Proverb.

48. Love is like war: easy to begin but hard to end
Meaning: Relationships can be complicated
.Origin: Russian Proverb.

49. A kind word is like a spring day
Meaning: Kindness makes life better.
Origin: Russian Proverb.

50. A man without a smiling face must not open a shop
Meaning: Good attitude is key to business success.
Origin: Chinese Proverb.

Chapter 31: 200 Famous Movie Lines

1."Here's looking at you, kid."
Movie: Casablanca
Character: Rick Blaine | Actor: Humphrey Bogart | Year: 1942

2."May the Force be with you."
Movie: Star Wars
Character: Various Characters | Actor: Multiple Actors | Year: 1977

3. "I'll be back."
Movie: The Terminator
Character: The Terminator | Actor: Arnold Schwarzenegger | Year: 1984

4."There's no place like home."
Movie: The Wizard of Oz
Character: Dorothy Gale | Actor: Judy Garland | Year: 1939

5."You can't handle the truth!"
Movie: A Few Good Men
Character: Col. Nathan R. Jessup | Actor: Jack Nicholson | Year: 1992

6."To infinity and beyond!"
Movie: Toy Story
Character: Buzz Lightyear | Actor: Tim Allen | Year: 1995

7."Life is like a box of chocolates."
Movie: Forrest Gump
Character: Forrest Gump | Actor: Tom Hanks | Year: 1994

8."I see dead people."
Movie: The Sixth Sense
Character: Cole Sear | Actor: Haley Joel Osment | Year: 1999

9."Why so serious?"
Movie: The Dark Knight
Character: The Joker | Actor: Heath Ledger | Year: 2008

10. "Say hello to my little friend!"
Movie: Scarface
Character: Tony Montana | Actor: Al Pacino | Year: 1983

11. "Frankly, my dear, I don't give a damn."
Movie: Gone with the Wind
Character: Rhett Butler | Actor: Clark Gable | Year: 1939

12. "I'm the king of the world!"
Movie: Titanic
Character: Jack Dawson | Actor: Leonardo DiCaprio | Year: 1997

13. "Keep your friends close, but your enemies closer."
Movie: The Godfather Part II
Character: Michael Corleone | Actor: Al Pacino | Year: 1974

14. "You talking to me?"
Movie: Taxi Driver
Character: Travis Bickle | Actor: Robert De Niro | Year: 1976

15. "E.T. phone home."
Movie: E.T. the Extra-Terrestrial
Character: E.T. | Actor: Pat Welsh (voice) | Year: 1982

16. "Show me the money!"
Movie: Jerry Maguire
Character: Rod Tidwell | Actor: Cuba Gooding Jr. | Year: 1996

17. "I feel the need—the need for speed."
Movie: Top Gun
Character: Maverick & Goose | Actor: Tom Cruise & Anthony Edwards | Year: 1986

18. "I'm gonna make him an offer he can't refuse."
Movie: The Godfather
Character: Vito Corleone | Actor: Marlon Brando | Year: 1972

19. "Houston, we have a problem."
Movie: Apollo 13
Character: Jim Lovell | Actor: Tom Hanks | Year: 1995

20."Hasta la vista, baby."

Movie: Terminator 2: Judgment Day
Character: The Terminator | Actor: Arnold Schwarzenegger | Year:
1991

21."They may take our lives, but they will never take our freedom!"

Movie: Braveheart
Character: William Wallace | Actor: Mel Gibson | Year: 1995

22."You had me at hello."

Movie: Jerry Maguire
Character: Dorothy Boyd | Actor: Renée Zellweger | Year: 1996

23."Bond. James Bond."

Movie: Dr. No
Character: James Bond | Actor: Sean Connery | Year: 1962

24."I love the smell of napalm in the morning."

Movie: Apocalypse Now
Character: Lt. Col. Bill Kilgore | Actor: Robert Duvall | Year: 1979

25."That'll do, pig. That'll do."

Movie: Babe
Character: Farmer Hoggett | Actor: James Cromwell | Year: 1995

26."Just keep swimming."

Movie: Finding Nemo
Character: Dory | Actor: Ellen DeGeneres | Year: 2003

27."There's no crying in baseball!"

Movie: A League of Their Own
Character: Jimmy Dugan | Actor: Tom Hanks | Year: 1992

28."You're gonna need a bigger boat."

Movie: Jaws
Character: Chief Brody | Actor: Roy Scheider | Year: 1975

29. "Roads? Where we're going, we don't need roads."
Movie: Back to the Future
Character: Dr. Emmett Brown | Actor: Christopher Lloyd | Year: 1985

30. "I'm as mad as hell, and I'm not going to take this anymore!"
Movie: Network
Character: Howard Beale | Actor: Peter Finch | Year: 1976

31. "A census taker once tried to test me. I ate his liver with some fava beans and a nice Chianti."
Movie: The Silence of the Lambs
Character: Dr. Hannibal Lecter | Actor: Anthony Hopkins | Year: 1991

32. "Stella! Hey, Stella!"
Movie: A Streetcar Named Desire
Character: Stanley Kowalski | Actor: Marlon Brando | Year: 1951

33. "Fasten your seatbelts. It's going to be a bumpy night."
Movie: All About Eve
Character: Margo Channing | Actor: Bette Davis | Year: 1950

34. "Play it, Sam. Play 'As Time Goes By.'"
Movie: Casablanca
Character: Ilsa Lund | Actor: Ingrid Bergman | Year: 1942

35. "I'm walking here! I'm walking here!"
Movie: Midnight Cowboy
Character: Ratso Rizzo | Actor: Dustin Hoffman | Year: 1969

36. "You know how to whistle, don't you, Steve? You just put your lips together and blow."
Movie: To Have and Have Not
Character: Marie 'Slim' Browning | Actor: Lauren Bacall | Year: 1944

37. "Why don't you come up sometime and see me?"
Movie: She Done Him Wrong
Character: Lady Lou | Actor: Mae West | Year: 1933

38. "I'm not bad. I'm just drawn that way."
Movie: Who Framed Roger Rabbit
Character: Jessica Rabbit | Actor: Kathleen Turner | Year: 1988

39. "My precious."
Movie: The Lord of the Rings: The Two Towers
Character: Gollum | Actor: Andy Serkis | Year: 2002

40. "Here's Johnny!"
Movie: The Shining
Character: Jack Torrance | Actor: Jack Nicholson | Year: 1980

41. "You can't fight in here! This is the War Room!"
Movie: Dr. Strangelove
Character: President Merkin Muffley | Actor: Peter Sellers | Year:

1964

42. "You is kind. You is smart. You is important."
Movie: The Help
Character: Aibileen Clark | Actor: Viola Davis | Year: 2011

43. "Keep the change, ya filthy animal."
Movie: Home Alone
Character: Gangster Johnny | Actor: Ralph Foody | Year: 1990

44. "Welcome to Jurassic Park."
Movie: Jurassic Park
Character: John Hammond | Actor: Richard Attenborough | Year: 1993

45. "Ohana means family. Family means nobody gets left behind."
Movie: Lilo & Stitch
Character: Stitch | Actor: Chris Sanders | Year: 2002

46. "I drink your milkshake!"
Movie: There Will Be Blood
Character: Daniel Plainview | Actor: Daniel Day-Lewis | Year: 2007

47."A boy's best friend is his mother."
Movie: Psycho
Character: Norman Bates | Actor: Anthony Perkins | Year: 1960

48. "We'll always have Paris."
Movie: Casablanca
Character: Rick Blaine | Actor: Humphrey Bogart | Year: 1942

49. "You either die a hero, or you live long enough to see yourself become the villain."
Movie: The Dark Knight
Character: Harvey Dent | Actor: Aaron Eckhart | Year: 2008

50. "That's all, folks!"
Movie: Looney Tunes
Character: Porky Pig | Actor: Mel Blanc | Year: 1930

51. "I live my life a quarter-mile at a time."
Movie: The Fast and the Furious
Character: Dominic Toretto | Actor: Vin Diesel | Year: 2001

52. "Help me, Obi-Wan Kenobi. You're my only hope."
Movie: Star Wars: A New Hope
Character: Princess Leia | Actor: Carrie Fisher | Year: 1977

53."Get busy living, or get busy dying."
Movie: The Shawshank Redemption
Character: Andy Dufresne | Actor: Tim Robbins | Year: 1994

54."You're tearing me apart, Lisa!"
Movie: The Room
Character: Johnny | Actor: Tommy Wiseau | Year: 2003

55."I see you."
Movie: Avatar
Character: Jake Sully | Actor: Sam Worthington | Year: 2009

56."This is Sparta!"
Movie: 300
Character: King Leonidas | Actor: Gerard Butler | Year: 2006

57. "You make me want to be a better man."
Movie: As Good as It Gets
Character: Melvin Udall | Actor: Jack Nicholson | Year: 1997

58. "Here's to looking at you, kid."
Movie: Casablanca
Character: Rick Blaine | Actor: Humphrey Bogart | Year: 1942

59. "I'm too old for this..."
Movie: Lethal Weapon
Character: Roger Murtaugh | Actor: Danny Glover | Year: 1987

60. "Looks like I picked the wrong week to quit sniffing glue."
Movie: Airplane!
Character: Steve McCroskey | Actor: Lloyd Bridges | Year: 1980\

61. "You met me at a very strange time in my life."
Movie: Fight Club
Character: Narrator | Actor: Edward Norton | Year: 1999

62. "I'm just one stomach flu away from my goal weight."
Movie: The Devil Wears Prada
Character: Emily Charlton | Actor: Emily Blunt | Year: 2006

63. "It's alive! It's alive!"
Movie: Frankenstein
Character: Henry Frankenstein | Actor: Colin Clive | Year: 1931

64. "Mama always said life was like a box of chocolates."
Movie: Forrest Gump
Character: Forrest Gump | Actor: Tom Hanks | Year: 1994

65. "You ain't heard nothin' yet!"
Movie: The Jazz Singer
Character: Jack Robin | Actor: Al Jolson | Year: 1927

66. "Oh, Jerry, don't let's ask for the moon. We have the stars."
Movie: Now Voyager
Character: Charlotte Vale |
Actor: Bette Davis | Year : 1942

67."Snakes. Why'd it have to be snakes?"
Movie: Raiders of the Lost Ark
Character: Indiana Jones | Actor: Harrison Ford | Year: 1981

68."Inconceivable!"
Movie: The Princess Bride
Character: Vizzini | Actor: Wallace Shawn | Year: 1987

69. "Why don't we just wait here for a little while... see what happens?"
Movie: The Thing
Character: MacReady | Actor: Kurt Russell | Year: 1982

70."Shaken, not stirred."
Movie: Goldfinger
Character: James Bond | Actor: Sean Connery | Year: 1964

71."It's not the years, honey. It's the mileage."
Movie: Raiders of the Lost Ark
Character: Indiana Jones | Actor: Harrison Ford | Year: 1981

72. "Life moves pretty fast. If you don't stop and look around once in a while, you could miss it."
Movie: Ferris Bueller's Day Off
Character: Ferris Bueller | Actor: Matthew Broderick | Year: 1986

73."I'm the Dude, so that's what you call me."
Movie: The Big Lebowski
Character: The Dude | Actor: Jeff Bridges | Year: 1998

74."I wish I knew how to quit you."
Movie: Brokeback Mountain
Character: Jack Twist | Actor: Jake Gyllenhaal | Year: 2005

75."That rug really tied the room together."
Movie: The Big Lebowski
Character: Walter Sobchak | Actor: John Goodman | Year: 1998

76."Toto, I've a feeling we're not in Kansas anymore."
Movie: The Wizard of Oz
Character: Dorothy Gale | Actor: Judy Garland | Year: 1939

77."Carpe diem. Seize the day, boys. Make your lives extraordinary."
Movie: Dead Poets Society
Character: John Keating | Actor: Robin Williams | Year: 1989

78."You're gonna need a bigger boat."
Movie: Jaws
Character: Martin Brody | Actor: Roy Scheider | Year: 1975

79."Wax on, wax off."
Movie: The Karate Kid
Character: Mr. Miyagi | Actor: Pat Morita | Year: 1984

80. "I am serious. And don't call me Shirley."
Movie: Airplane!
Character: Dr. Rumack | Actor: Leslie Nielsen | Year: 1980

81."If you build it, he will come."
Movie: Field of Dreams
Character: The Voice | Actor: Ray Liotta | Year: 1989

82."I'm Batman."
Movie: Batman Begins
Character: Bruce Wayne | Actor: Christian Bale | Year: 2005

83."Chewie, we're home."
Movie: Star Wars: The Force Awakens
Character: Han Solo | Actor: Harrison Ford | Year: 2015

84."It's clobberin' time!"
Movie: Fantastic Four
Character: The Thing | Actor: Michael Chiklis | Year: 2005

85. "Great Scott!"
Movie: Back to the Future
Character: Dr. Emmett Brown | Actor: Christopher Lloyd | Year: 1985

86. "The first rule of Fight Club is: You do not talk about Fight Club."
Movie: Fight Club
Character: Tyler Durden | Actor: Brad Pitt | Year: 1999

87. "That's one small step for man, one giant leap for mankind."
Movie: First Man
Character: Neil Armstrong | Actor: Ryan Gosling | Year: 2018

88. "I'm just a girl, standing in front of a boy, asking him to love her."
Movie: Notting Hill
Character: Anna Scott | Actor: Julia Roberts | Year: 1999

89. "Keep moving forward."
Movie: Meet the Robinsons
Character: Wilbur Robinson | Actor: Wesley Singerman | Year: 2007

90. "Freedom!"
Movie: Braveheart
Character: William Wallace | Actor: Mel Gibson | Year: 1995

91. "Every time a bell rings, an angel gets his wings."
Movie: It's a Wonderful Life
Character: Zuzu Bailey | Actor: Karolyn Grimes | Year: 1946

92. "You're a wizard, Harry."
Movie: Harry Potter and the Sorcerer's Stone
Character: Hagrid | Actor: Robbie Coltrane | Year: 2001

93. "It's not who I am underneath, but what I do that defines me."
Movie: Batman Begins
Character: Bruce Wayne | Actor: Christian Bale | Year: 2005

94."Go the distance."
Movie: Field of Dreams
Character: Shoeless Joe Jackson | Actor: Ray Liotta | Year: 198z

95."With great power comes great responsibility."
Movie: Spider-Man
Character: Uncle Ben | Actor: Cliff Robertson | Year: 2002

96."Do, or do not. There is no try."
Movie: Star Wars: The Empire Strikes Back
Character: Yoda | Actor: Frank Oz | Year: 1980

97."No, I am your father."
Movie: Star Wars: The Empire Strikes Back
Character: Darth Vader | Actor: David Prowse (voiced by James Earl Jones) | Year: 1980

98."Elementary, my dear Watson."
Movie: The Adventures of Sherlock Holmes
Character: Sherlock Holmes | Actor: Basil Rathbone | Year: 1939

99. "That's no moon. It's a space station."
Movie: Star Wars: A New Hope
Character: Obi-Wan Kenobi | Actor: Alec Guinness | Year: 1977

100."I'm having an old friend for dinner."
Movie: The Silence of the Lambs
Character: Hannibal Lecter | Actor: Anthony Hopkins | Year: 1991

101."Show me the meaning of haste!"
Movie: The Lord of the Rings: The Two Towers
Character: Gandalf | Actor: Ian McKellen | Year: 2002

102."I volunteer as tribute!"
Movie: The Hunger Games
Character: Katniss Everdeen | Actor: Jennifer Lawrence | Year: 2012

103."Some people are worth melting for."
Movie: Frozen
Character: Olaf | Actor: Josh Gad | Year: 2013

104."Remember, remember the Fifth of November."
Movie: V for Vendetta
Character: V | Actor: Hugo Weaving | Year: 2005

105."There's a snake in my boot!"
Movie: Toy Story
Character: Woody | Actor: Tom Hanks | Year: 199

106."The cold never bothered me anyway."
Movie: Frozen
Character: Elsa | Actor: Idina Menzel | Year: 2013

107."I'm gonna wreck it!"
Movie: Wreck-It Ralph
Character: Ralph | Actor: John C. Reilly | Year: 2012

108."Why is the rum gone?"
Movie: Pirates of the Caribbean: The Curse of the Black Pearl
Character: Jack Sparrow | Actor: Johnny Depp | Year: 2003

109."This is the way."
Movie: The Mandalorian
Character: Din Djarin | Actor: Pedro Pascal | Year: 2019

110."We are Groot."
Movie: Guardians of the Galaxy
Character: Groot | Actor: Vin Diesel | Year: 2014

111. "I'll never let go, Jack. I'll never let go."
Movie: Titanic
Character: Rose | Actor: Kate Winslet | Year: 1997

112."I solemnly swear that I am up to no good."
Movie: Harry Potter and the Prisoner of Azkaban
Character: Fred & George Weasley | Actor: James & Oliver Phelps |
Year: 2004

113."You complete me."
Movie: Jerry Maguire
Character: Jerry Maguire | Actor: Tom Cruise | Year: 1996

114."Some men just want to watch the world burn."
Movie: The Dark Knight
Character: Alfred | Actor: Michael Caine | Year: 2008

115."Ogres are like onions."
Movie: Shrek
Character: Shrek | Actor: Mike Myers | Year: 2001

116."I am your father."
Movie: Star Wars: The Empire Strikes Back
Character: Darth Vader | Actor: David Prowse (voiced by James Earl Jones) | Year: 1980

117. "That's not a knife. This is a knife."
Movie: Crocodile Dundee
Character: Mick Dundee | Actor: Paul Hogan | Year: 1986

118."Say 'hello' to my little friend!"
Movie: Scarface
Character: Tony Montana | Actor: Al Pacino | Year: 1983

119."They call it a Royale with Cheese."
Movie: Pulp Fiction
Character: Vincent Vega | Actor: John Travolta | Year: 1994

120. "You can't handle the truth!"
Movie: A Few Good Men
Character: Col. Nathan R. Jessup | Actor: Jack Nicholson | Year: 1992

121. "My mama always said, 'Life was like a box of chocolates. You never know what you're gonna get.'"
Movie: Forrest Gump
Character: Forrest Gump | Actor: Tom Hanks | Year: 1994

122. "That'll do, pig. That'll do."
Movie: Babe
Character: Farmer Hoggett | Actor: James Cromwell | Year: 1995

123. "We rob banks."
Movie: Bonnie and Clyde
Character: Clyde Barrow | Actor: Warren Beatty | Year: 1967

124. "Yo, Adrian!"
Movie: Rocky
Character: Rocky Balboa | Actor: Sylvester Stallone | Year: 1976

125. "Why don't you come up sometime and see me?"
Movie: She Done Him Wrong
Character: Lady Lou | Actor: Mae West | Year: 1933

126. "Nobody puts Baby in a corner."
Movie: Dirty Dancing
Character: Johnny Castle | Actor: Patrick Swayze | Year: 1987

127. "Fasten your seatbelts. It's going to be a bumpy night."
Movie: All About Eve
Character: Margo Channing | Actor: Bette Davis | Year: 1950

128. "A boy's best friend is his mother."
Movie: Psycho
Character: Norman Bates | Actor: Anthony Perkins | Year: 1960

129. "Just when I thought I was out, they pull me back in!"
Movie: The Godfather Part III
Character: Michael Corleone | Actor: Al Pacino | Year: 1990

130. "This is my rifle. There are many like it, but this one is mine."
Movie: Full Metal Jacket
Character: Gunnery Sgt. Hartman | Actor: R. Lee Ermey | Year: 1987

131. "You're killin' me, Smalls!"
Movie: The Sandlot
Character: Ham Porter | Actor: Patrick Renna | Year: 1993

132. "It's just a flesh wound."
Movie: Monty Python and the Holy Grail
Character: Black Knight | Actor: John Cleese | Year: 1975

133. "Leave the gun. Take the cannoli."
Movie: The Godfather
Character: Peter Clemenza | Actor: Richard S. Castellano | Year: 1972

134. "You got knocked the f*** out!"
Movie: Friday
Character: Smokey | Actor: Chris Tucker | Year: 1995

135. "Molly, you in danger girl."
Movie: Ghost
Character: Oda Mae Brown | Actor: Whoopi Goldberg | Year: 1990

136. "If you're a bird, I'm a bird."
Movie: The Notebook
Character: Noah | Actor: Ryan Gosling | Year: 2004

137. "I have had it with these motherf***ing snakes on this motherf***ing plane!"
Movie: Snakes on a Plane
Character: Neville Flynn | Actor: Samuel L. Jackson | Year: 2006

138. "What is this? A center for ants?"
Movie: Zoolander
Character: Derek Zoolander | Actor: Ben Stiller | Year: 2001

139. "That's the Chicago way!"
Movie: The Untouchables
Character: Jim Malone | Actor: Sean Connery | Year: 1987

140. "It's called a hustle, sweetheart."
Movie: Zootopia
Character: Nick Wilde | Actor: Jason Bateman | Year: 2016

141. "Do you want to build a snowman?"
Movie: Frozen
Character: Anna | Actor: Kristen Bell | Year: 2013

142. "I'm not even supposed to be here today!"
Movie: Clerks
Character: Dante Hicks | Actor: Brian O'Halloran | Year: 1994

143. "To me, you are perfect."
Movie: Love Actually
Character: Mark | Actor: Andrew Lincoln | Year: 2003

144. "We are the music makers, and we are the dreamers of dreams."
Movie: Willy Wonka & the Chocolate Factory
Character: Willy Wonka | Actor: Gene Wilder | Year: 1971

145. "You know, for kids!"
Movie: The Hudsucker Proxy
Character: Sidney J. Mussburger | Actor: Paul Newman | Year: 1994

146. "Oh, what a day… what a lovely day!"
Movie: Mad Max: Fury Road
Character: Nux | Actor: Nicholas Hoult | Year: 2015

147. "I have a very particular set of skills."
Movie: Taken
Character: Bryan Mills | Actor: Liam Neeson | Year: 2008

148. "Gentlemen, you can't fight in here! This is the War Room!"
Movie: Dr. Strangelove
Character: President Merkin Muffley | Actor: Peter Sellers | Year: 1964

149. "I don't want to survive. I want to live."
Movie: 12 Years a Slave
Character: Solomon Northup | Actor: Chiwetel Ejiofor | Year: 2013

150. "You mustn't be afraid to dream a little bigger, darling."
Movie: Inception
Character: Eames | Actor: Tom Hardy | Year: 2010

151. "That's the sound of inevitability."
Movie: The Matrix
Character: Agent Smith | Actor: Hugo Weaving | Year: 1999

152. "I'm funny how? I mean funny like I'm a clown? I amuse you?"
Movie: Goodfellas
Character: Tommy DeVito | Actor: Joe Pesci | Year: 1990

153. "You either die a hero or live long enough to see yourself become the villain."
Movie: The Dark Knight
Character: Harvey Dent | Actor: Aaron Eckhart | Year: 2008

154. "I am inevitable."
Movie: Avengers: Endgame
Character: Thanos | Actor: Josh Brolin | Year: 2019

155. "Wakanda forever!"
Movie: Black Panther
Character: T'Challa | Actor: Chadwick Boseman | Year: 2018

156. "I wish there was a way to know you're in the good old days before you've actually left them."
Movie: The Office
Character: Andy Bernard | Actor: Ed Helms | Year: 2013

157. "You shall not pass!"
Movie: The Lord of the Rings: The Fellowship of the Ring
Character: Gandalf | Actor: Ian McKellen | Year: 2001

158. "I know kung fu."
Movie: The Matrix
Character: Neo | Actor: Keanu Reeves | Year: 1999

159. "You sit on a throne of lies."
Movie: Elf
Character: Buddy | Actor: Will Ferrell | Year: 2003

160. "It's a trap!"
Movie: Star Wars: Return of the Jedi
Character: Admiral Ackbar | Actor: Erik Bauersfeld | Year: 1983

161. "I don't know who you are. I don't know what you want."
Movie: Taken
Character: Bryan Mills | Actor: Liam Neeson | Year: 2008

162. "You had my curiosity, but now you have my attention."
Movie: Django Unchained
Character: Calvin Candie | Actor: Leonardo DiCaprio | Year: 2012 \

163. "It was beauty killed the beast."
Movie: King Kong
Character: Carl Denham | Actor: Robert Armstrong | Year: 1933

164. "I've always depended on the kindness of strangers."
Movie: A Streetcar Named Desire
Character: Blanche DuBois | Actor: Vivien Leigh | Year: 1951

165. "Put some Windex on it."
Movie: My Big Fat Greek Wedding
Character: Gus Portokalos | Actor: Michael Constantine | Year: 2002

166. "Oh captain, my captain."
Movie: Dead Poets Society
Character: Students | Actor: Various | Year: 1989

167. "Snap out of it!"
Movie: Moonstruck
Character: Loretta Castorini | Actor: Cher | Year: 1987

168. "You were the chosen one!"
Movie: Star Wars: Revenge of the Sith
Character: Obi-Wan Kenobi | Actor: Ewan McGregor | Year: 2005

169."Do you feel lucky, punk?"
Movie: Dirty Harry
Character: Harry Callahan | Actor: Clint Eastwood | Year: 1971

170. "I am big! It's the pictures that got small."
Movie: Sunset Boulevard
Character: Norma Desmond | Actor: Gloria Swanson | Year: 1950

171. "It's alive! It's alive!"
Movie: Frankenstein
Character: Henry Frankenstein | Actor: Colin Clive | Year: 1931

172. "I do wish we could chat longer, but I'm having an old friend for dinner."
Movie: The Silence of the Lambs
Character: Hannibal Lecter | Actor: Anthony Hopkins | Year: 1991

173. "Get your stinking paws off me, you damned dirty ape!"
Movie: Planet of the Apes
Character: George Taylor | Actor: Charlton Heston | Year: 1968

174."I coulda been a contender."
Movie: On the Waterfront
Character: Terry Malloy | Actor: Marlon Brando | Year: 1954

175."Play it again, Sam."
Movie: Casablanca
Character: Ilsa Lund | Actor: Ingrid Bergman | Year: 1942

176. "It's not the years, honey. It's the mileage."
Movie: Raiders of the Lost Ark
Character: Indiana Jones | Actor: Harrison Ford | Year: 1981

177. "I'm the king of the world!"
Movie: Titanic
Character: Jack Dawson | Actor: Leonardo DiCaprio | Year: 1997

178. "There's no place like home."
Movie: The Wizard of Oz
Character: Dorothy Gale | Actor: Judy Garland | Year: 1939

179. "Toto, I've a feeling we're not in Kansas anymore."
Movie: The Wizard of Oz
Character: Dorothy Gale | Actor: Judy Garland | Year: 1939

180. "May the Force be with you."
Movie: Star Wars
Character: Obi-Wan Kenobi | Actor: Alec Guinness | Year: 1977

181. "I am serious. And don't call me Shirley."
Movie: Airplane!
Character: Dr. Rumack | Actor: Leslie Nielsen | Year: 1980

182. "You shall not pass!"
Movie: The Lord of the Rings: The Fellowship of the Ring
Character: Gandalf | Actor: Ian McKellen | Year: 2001

183. "To infinity and beyond!"
Movie: Toy Story
Character: Buzz Lightyear | Actor: Tim Allen | Year: 1995

184. "Open the pod bay doors, HAL."
Movie: 2001: A Space Odyssey
Character: Dave Bowman | Actor: Keir Dullea | Year: 1968

185. "I see you."
Movie: Avatar
Character: Jake Sully | Actor: Sam Worthington | Year: 2009

186. "I'll be back."
Movie: The Terminator
Character: The Terminator | Actor: Arnold Schwarzenegger | Year: 1984

187. "It's clobberin' time!"
Movie: Fantastic Four
Character: The Thing | Actor: Michael Chiklis | Year: 2005

188. "Go ahead, make my day."
Movie: Sudden Impact
Character: Harry Callahan | Actor: Clint Eastwood | Year: 1983

189. "Help me, Obi-Wan Kenobi. You're my only hope."
Movie: Star Wars: A New Hope
Character: Princess Leia | Actor: Carrie Fisher | Year: 1977

190."Why so serious?"
Movie: The Dark Knight
Character: The Joker | Actor: Heath Ledger | Year: 2008

191."I'm the king of the world!"
Movie: Titanic
Character: Jack Dawson | Actor: Leonardo DiCaprio | Year: 1997

192."Some people are worth melting for."
Movie: Frozen
Character: Olaf | Actor: Josh Gad | Year: 2013

193."Say hello to my little friend!"
Movie: Scarface
Character: Tony Montana | Actor: Al Pacino | Year: 1983

194. "I'm just a girl, standing in front of a boy, asking him to love her."
Movie: Notting Hill
Character: Anna Scott | Actor: Julia Roberts | Year: 1999

195. "I wish there was a way to know you're in the good old days before you've actually left them."
Movie: The Office
Character: Andy Bernard | Actor: Ed Helms | Year: 2013

196."You got knocked the f*** out!"
Movie: Friday
Character: Smokey | Actor: Chris Tucker | Year: 1995

197. "You met me at a very strange time in my life."
Movie: Fight Club
Character: Narrator | Actor: Edward Norton | Year: 1999

198. "You can't fight in here! This is the War Room!"
Movie: Dr. Strangelove
Character: President Merkin Muffley | Actor: Peter Sellers | Year: 1964

199. "I'm gonna make him an offer he can't refuse."
Movie: The Godfather
Character: Vito Corleone | Actor: Marlon Brando | Year: 1972

200. "This is Sparta!"
Movie: 300
Character: King Leonidas | Actor: Gerard Butler | Year: 2006

Chapter 32: Famous Latin & Foreign Phrases (With Phonetics)

1."Carpe diem" (Latin)
Meaning: Seize the day.
Origin: Latin

2."Veni, vidi, vici" (Latin)
Meaning: I came, I saw, I conquered.
Origin: Latin

3."C'est la vie" (French)
Meaning: That's life.
Origin: French

4."Hasta la vista" (Spanish)
Meaning: See you later.
Origin: Terminator: Arnold Schwarzengegger

5."Je ne sais quoi" (French)
Meaning: A certain indescribable quality.
Origin: I know not what French

6."Amor fati" (Latin)
Meaning: Love of fate.
Origin: Unknown

7."Memento mori" (Latin)
Meaning: Remember that you will die.
Origin: Unknown

8."Eureka!" (Greek)
Meaning: I have found it!
Origin: Unknown

9."Alea iacta est" (Latin)
Meaning: The die is cast.
Origin: Unknown

10."Schadenfreude" (German)
Meaning: Pleasure derived from another's misfortune.
Origin: Unknown

11."Dolce far niente" (Italian)
Meaning: The sweetness of doing nothing.
Origin: Unknown

12."Joie de vivre" (French)
Meaning: Joy of living.
Origin: Unknown

13."In vino veritas" (Latin)
Meaning: In wine, there is truth.
Origin: Pliny the Elder

14."Modus operandi" (Latin)
Meaning: Method of operating.
Origin: Unknown

15."Quid pro quo" (Latin)
Meaning: Something for something.
Origin: Unknown

16."Tempus fugit" (Latin)
Meaning: Time flies.
Origin: Unknown

17."Caveat emptor" (Latin)
Meaning: Let the buyer beware.
Origin: Latin

18."Habeas corpus" (Latin)
Meaning: You shall have the body (legal term).
Origin: Unknown

19."Per aspera ad astra" (Latin)
Meaning: Through hardships to the stars.
Origin: Unknown

20."Non plus ultra" (Latin)
Meaning: The ultimate, the best.
Origin: Unknown

21."Ad astra per aspera" (Latin)
Meaning: To the stars through difficulties.
Origin: Unknown

22."Fiat lux" (Latin)
Meaning: Let there be light.
Origin:Bible

23."A priori" (Latin)
Meaning: Knowledge that comes before experience.
Origin: Unknown

24."Acta non verba" (Latin)
Meaning: Actions, not words.
Origin: Unknown

25."C'est la guerre" (French)
Meaning: Such is war.
Origin: Unknown

26."Schadenfreude" (German)
Meaning: Enjoyment of others' misfortune.
Origin: German

27."L'esprit de l'escalier" (French)
Meaning: Thinking of the perfect reply too late.
Origin: Unknown

28."Deus ex machina" (Latin)
Meaning: An unexpected power saving a situation.
Origin: Unknown

29."Amor vincit omnia" (Latin)
Meaning: Love conquers all.
Origin: Unknown

30."Errare humanum est" (Latin)
Meaning: To err is human.
Origin: Unknown

\

31."Non sequitur" (Latin)
Meaning: A statement that does not logically follow.
Origin: Unknown

32."Fait accompli" (French)
Meaning: Something already completed.
Origin: Unknown

33."Viva la revolución" (Spanish)
Meaning: Long live the revolution.
Origin: Unknown

34."Per diem" (Latin)
Meaning: By the day.
Origin: Unknown

35."Status quo" (Latin)
Meaning: The existing state of affairs.
Origin: Latin

36."Sic semper tyrannis" (Latin)
Meaning: Thus always to tyrants.
Origin: Unknown

37."Dum spiro spero" (Latin)
Meaning: While I breathe, I hope.
Origin: Unknown

38."Semper fidelis" (Latin)
Meaning: Always faithful.
Origin: Unknown

39."Amor patriae" (Latin)
Meaning: Love of country.
Origin: Unknown

40."Cogito, ergo sum" (Latin)
Meaning: I think, therefore I am.
Origin: Unknown

41."Omnia vincit amor" (Latin)
Meaning: Love conquers all.
Origin: Unknown

42."Alea jacta est" (Latin)
Meaning: The die is cast.
Origin: Unknown

43."Audentes fortuna iuvat" (Latin)
Meaning: Fortune favors the bold.
Origin: Unknown

44. "Per ardua ad astra" (Latin)
Meaning: Through adversity to the stars.
Origin: Unknown

45. "Fiat voluntas tua" (Latin)
Meaning: Let your will be done.
Origin: Unknown

46. "Nil desperandum" (Latin)
Meaning: Never despair.
Origin: Unknown

47. "Carpe noctem" (Latin)
Meaning: Seize the night.
Origin: Unknown

48. "Lupus in fabula" (Latin)
Meaning: Speak of the wolf, and he shall appear.
Origin: Unknown

49. "Ad hoc" (Latin)
Meaning: For this purpose only.
Origin: Unknown

50. "Memento vivere" (Latin)
Meaning: Remember to live.
Origin: Unknown

51. "Sapere aude" (Latin)
Meaning: Dare to know.
Origin: Unknown

52. "Felix culpa" (Latin)
Meaning: Happy fault.
Origin: Unknown

53."Non compos mentis" (Latin)
Meaning: Not of sound mind.
Oriigin: Unknown

54."C'est magnifique" (French)
Meaning: It's magnificent.
Origin: French Phrase

55."Je suis désolé" (French)
Meaning: I am sorry.
Origin: French phrase

56."Que será, será" (Spanish)
Meaning: What will be, will be.
Origin: Italian phrase che sara

57."Mi casa es su casa" (Spanish)
Meaning: My house is your house.
Origin: Spanish

58."Merci beaucoup" (French)
Meaning: Thank you very much.
Origin: French

59."Bon appétit" (French)
Meaning: Enjoy your meal
. Origin: French

60."Guten Tag" (German)
Meaning: Good day.
Origin: German

61."Hasta luego" (Spanish)
Meaning: See you later.
Origin: Spanish

62."Prost!" (German) Meaning: Cheers!
Meaning: Cheers!
Origin: Unknown

63."Buona fortuna" (Italian)
Meaning: Good luck.
Origin: Unknown

64."Arrivederci" (Italian)
Meaning: Goodbye.
Origin: Unknown

65."Tutto bene" (Italian)
Meaning: Everything is fine.
Origin: Unknown

66."Por favor" (Spanish)
Meaning: Please.
Origin: Unknown

67."Lo siento" (Spanish)
Meaning: I'm sorry.
Origin: Unknown

68."Buongiorno" (Italian)
Meaning: Good morning.
Origin: Unknown

69."Ça va?" (French)
Meaning: How's it going?
Origin: French

70."Comment ça va?" (French)
Meaning: How are you?
 Origin: French

71."Bonne nuit" (French)
Meaning: Good night.
Origin: Unknown

72."Grazie mille" (Italian)
Meaning: Thank you very much.
Origin: Unknown

73."De nada" (Spanish)
Meaning: You're welcome.
Origin: Unknown

74."Bitte" (German)
Meaning: Please or you're welcome.
Origin: Unknown

75."Guten Abend" (German)
Meaning: Good evening.
Origin: Unknown

76."Bonne chance" (French)
Meaning: Good luck.
Origin: Unknown

77."Tschüss" (German)
Meaning: Bye!
Origin: Unknown

78."Por qué?" (Spanish)
Meaning: Why?
Origin: Unknown

79."Wie geht's?" (German)
 Meaning: How are you?
Origin: Unknown

80."Danke schön" (German)
Meaning: Thank you very much.
Origin: Unknown

81."Mon dieu!" (French)
Meaning: My God!
Origin: Unknown

82."Mi amor" (Spanish)
Meaning: My love.
Origin: Unknown

83."Salut!" (French)
Meaning: Hi! or Cheers!
Origin: Unknown

84."Ciao!" (Italian)
Meaning: Hello or Goodbye.
Origin: Unknown

85."Bis später" (German)
Meaning: See you later.
Origin: Unknown

86."Parlez-vous anglais?" (French)
Meaning: Do you speak English?
Origin: Unknown

87."J'adore" (French)
Meaning: I love it.
Origin: Unknown

88."Buona notte" (Italian)
Meaning: Good night.
Origin: Unknown

89."Merde!" (French)
Meaning: Damn!
Origin: Unknown

90."Ti amo" (Italian)
Meaning: I love you.
Origin: Unknown

91."Allez!" (French)
Meaning: Go!
Origin: Unknown

92."Bon voyage" (French)
Meaning: Have a good trip.
Origin: Unknown

93."À bientôt" (French)
Meaning: See you soon.
Origin: Unknown

94."Ça ne fait rien" (French)
Meaning: It doesn't matter.
Origin: Unknown

95."Buon viaggio" (Italian)
Meaning: Good journey.
Origin: Unknown

96."Buona giornata" (Italian)
Meaning: Have a nice day.
Origin: Unknown

97."Laissez-faire" (French)
Meaning: Let it be (hands-off approach).
Origin: French

98."Aut viam inveniam aut faciam" (Latin)
Meaning: I shall either find a way or make one.
Origin: Unknown

99."Fiat justitia ruat caelum" (Latin)
Meaning: Let justice be done, though the heavens fall.
Origin: Unknown

100."Non e un problema"(Italian)
Meaning : Please
Origin : Unknown

End of Chapter 32

Chapter 33: Modern Lingo & Slang (200 Phrases with Origins)

1."YOLO"
Meaning: You Only Live Once.
Origin: Slang

2."FOMO"
Meaning: Fear Of Missing Out.
Origin: Slang

3."GOAT"
Meaning: Greatest Of All Time.
Origin: Slang

4."Flex"
Meaning: To show off.
Origin: Slang

5."Lit"
Meaning: Exciting or excellent.
Origin: Slang

6."Vibe check"
Meaning: Assessing the mood or energy of a situation.
Origin: Slang

7."Ghosting"
Meaning: Suddenly cutting off communication.
Origin: Slang

8."Clout"
Meaning: Influence or fame.
Origin: Slang

9."Tea"
Meaning: Gossip or juicy details.
Origin: Slang

10."Shook"
Meaning: Deeply affected or shocked.
Origin: Slang

11."Binge-watch"
Meaning: Watching multiple episodes in one sitting.
Origin: Slang

12."Low-key"
Meaning: Something subtle or not overly expressed.
Origin: Slang

13."High-key"
Meaning: Something obvious or strongly felt.
Origin: Slang

14."Sus"
Meaning: Suspicious or questionable.
Origin: Slang

15."Stan"
Meaning: Overly enthusiastic fan.
Origin: Slang

16."Salty"
Meaning: Bitter or upset about something.
Origin: Slang

17."Slay"
Meaning: To do something exceptionally well.
Origin: Slang

18."Main character energy"
Meaning: Confidence like a movie protagonist.
Origin: Slang

19."Glow up"
Meaning: Significant transformation for the better.
Origin: Slang

20."No cap"
Meaning: For real, no lie.
Origin: Slang

21."Big yikes"
Meaning: An even bigger embarrassment than 'yikes'.
Origin: Slang

22."Snack"
Meaning: Someone attractive.
Origin: Slang

23."Clap back"
Meaning: A sharp, witty response.
Origin: Slang

24."Bet"
Meaning: Another way of saying 'okay' or 'watch me'.
Origin: Slang

25."Receipts"
Meaning: Proof of an action, often screenshots.
Origin: Slang

26."Hits different"
Meaning: Feels unique or special compared to usual
Origin: Unknown.

27."Simp"
Meaning: Someone who does way too much for someone they like.
Origin: Slang

28."Living rent-free"
Meaning: Something constantly in your mind.
Origin: Slang

29."Finna"
Meaning: Short for 'fixing to' or 'going to'.
Origin: Slang

30."Gucci"
Meaning: Everything is good or cool.
Origin: Slang

31."Drip"
Meaning: Stylish clothing or accessories.
Origin: Slang

32."Mid"
Meaning: Mediocre, nothing special.
Origin: Slang

33."Stan"
Meaning: A dedicated fan, from Eminem's song 'Stan'.
Origin: Slang

34."Mood"
Meaning: Relatable feeling or emotion.
Origin: Slang

35."Vibing"
Meaning: Enjoying the moment, feeling good.
Origin: Slang

36. "Bae"
Meaning: A term of endearment for a significant other.
Origin: Slang

37. "Throw shade"
Meaning: To subtly insult someone.
Origin: African American Vernacular English (AAVE)

38. "Woke"
Meaning: Being socially aware.
Origin: AAVE/Social Justice Movement

39. "Yeet"
Meaning: To throw something forcefully or express excitement.
Origin: Slang

40. "Flex"
Meaning: To show off.
Origin: Hip-Hop Culture

41. "Receipts"
Meaning: Proof of something happening, often in the form of screenshots. Origin: Slang

42. "Clout"
Meaning: Influence or fame.
Origin: Hip-Hop Culture

43. "No cap"
Meaning: No lie, being serious.
Origin: Slang

44. "Bet"
Meaning: Used to confirm or agree with something.
Origin: Slang

45."Salty"
Meaning: Being upset or bitter about something.
Origin: AAVE/Gaming Community

46."Ghosting"
Meaning: Suddenly cutting off communication.
Origin: Slang

47."Simp"
Meaning: Someone overly attentive to someone they admire.
Origin: Slang

48."Big mood"
Meaning: A strong relatable feeling.
Origin: Slang

49."Low-key"
Meaning: Something subtle or understated.
Origin: Slang

50."High-key"
Meaning: Something obvious or strongly felt.
Origin: Slang

51."Shook"
Meaning: Deeply affected or shocked.
Origin: Slang

52."Vibe check"
Meaning: Assessing the mood or energy of a person or place.
Origin: Slang

53."FOMO"
Meaning: Fear of Missing Out.
Origin: Slang

54."YOLO"
Meaning: You Only Live Once.
Origin: Hip-Hop Culture (Popularized by Drake)

55."Stan"
Meaning: An overly enthusiastic fan.
Origin: Eminem's Song 'Stan' (2000)

56."Sus"
Meaning: Suspicious or questionable.
Origin: AAVE/Gaming Community (Among Us)

57."Main character energy"
Meaning: Acting with confidence like the protagonist of a movie.
Origin: TikTok/Pop Culture

58."Binge-watch"
Meaning: Watching multiple episodes in one sitting.
Origin: Streaming Culture

59."Karen"
Meaning: A stereotype for an entitled, complaining person.
Origin: Slang

60."Gaslight"
Meaning: Manipulating someone into questioning their reality.
Origin: Psychology/Popular Culture

61."Glow up"
Meaning: A significant transformation for the better.
Origin: Slang

62."Slay"
Meaning: To do something exceptionally well.
Origin: LGBTQ+ & Drag Community

63. "Basic"
Meaning: Liking mainstream or cliché things.
Origin: Slang

64. "Cancelled"
Meaning: Boycotted or rejected due to past behavior.
Origin: Social Media/Twitter

65. "Drip"
Meaning: Stylish clothing or accessories.
Origin: Hip-Hop Culture

66. "Thirsty"
Meaning: Desperate for attention.
Origin: Slang

67. "Hits different"
Meaning: Feels unique or special compared to usual.
Origin: Slang

68. "Cap"
Meaning: A lie.
Origin: AAVE/Hip-Hop Culture

69. "Finna"
Meaning: Short for 'fixing to' or 'going to'.
Origin: AAVE/Southern U.S.

70. "Gucci"
Meaning: Everything is good or cool.
Origin: Hip-Hop Culture

71. "Tea"
Meaning: Gossip or juicy details.
Origin: LGBTQ+ & Drag Community

72."Lit"
Meaning: Exciting or excellent.
Origin: Hip-Hop Culture

73."Snack"
Meaning: Someone attractive.
Origin: Slang

74."Pressed"
Meaning: Upset or bothered.
Origin: Slang

75."Dead"
Meaning: Something is so funny it 'killed' you.
Origin: Slang

76."Living rent-free"
Meaning: Something constantly in your mind.
Origin: Slang

77."Soft launch"
Meaning: Subtly revealing a new relationship online.
Origin: Slang

78."Clap back"
Meaning: A sharp, witty response.
Origin: AAVE/Hip-Hop Culture

79."Ratio"
Meaning: When a reply gets more likes than the original tweet.
Origin: Slang

80."Left on read"
Meaning: Someone reads a message but doesn't reply.
Origin: Slang

81."Big yikes"
Meaning: An even bigger embarrassment than 'yikes'.
Origin: Slang

82."Cheugy"
Meaning: Outdated or trying too hard.
Origin: Slang

83."Sksksk"
Meaning: Expressing excitement or laughter.
Origin: TikTok/VSCO Girl Culture

84."Periodt"
Meaning: Used to emphasize a point.
Origin: Slang

85."Deadass"
Meaning: Completely serious.
Origin: Slang

86."Smol"
Meaning: Something cute and small.
Origin: Slang

87."Pog"
Meaning: Exciting or cool, from Twitch.
Origin: Slang

88."Mid"
Meaning: Mediocre, nothing special.

89."Chad"
Meaning: A confident, stereotypically attractive male.
Origin: Slang

90."Doomscrolling"
Meaning: Endlessly consuming negative news online.
Origin: Slang

91."Stan Twitter"
Meaning: A section of Twitter with intense fan bases.
Origin: Slang

92."Sheesh"
Meaning: Expressing amazement or disbelief.
Origin: Slang

93."Based"
Meaning: Being true to yourself, not caring about opinions.
Origin: Slang

94."No thoughts, head empty"
Meaning: Describes a blank or carefree mindset.
Origin: Slang

95."We move"
Meaning: Accepting a bad situation and moving forward.
Origin: Slang

96."Rent free"
Meaning: When something stays in your mind.
Origin: Slang

97."It's giving..."
Meaning: Describing the vibe or impression something has.
Origin: Slang

98."Gatekeeping"
Meaning: Withholding knowledge to keep something exclusive.
Origin: Slang

99."Touch grass"
Meaning: Telling someone to go outside and get off the internet.
Origin: Slang

100."Sigma male"
Meaning: A lone-wolf, non-conformist man.
Origin: Red Pill/Manosphere Culture

101."Mansplain"
Meaning: A man explaining something in a condescending way.
Origin: Slang

102."Skrrt"
Meaning: Sound effect representing a quick departure.
Origin: Hip-Hop Culture

103."Bruh moment"
Meaning: A ridiculous or dumb situation.
Origin: Slang

104."Ate and left no crumbs"
Meaning: Did something flawlessly.
Origin: Slang

105."Spill the tea"
Meaning: Tell the gossip.
Origin: Slang

106."Sending it"
Meaning: Going all out with no hesitation.

107."Side-eye"
Meaning: A look of suspicion or disapproval.
Origin: Slang

108."Rizz"
Meaning: Charisma or ability to flirt successfully.
Origin: Slang

109."Vibe"
Meaning: The mood or atmosphere of a situation.
Origin: Slang

110."Dap"
Meaning: A friendly handshake or greeting.
Origin: AAVE/Hip-Hop Culture

111."Mood"
Meaning: A relatable feeling.
Origin: Slang

112."Slaps"
Meaning: Something that is really good.
Origin: Slang

113."Wildin'"
Meaning: Acting crazy or out of control.
Origin: Slang

114."L"
Meaning: Taking a loss or failure.
Origin: Slang

115."W"
Meaning: A win or success.

116."Dank"
Meaning: High quality or impressive, often used for memes.
Origin: Slang

117."Troll"
Meaning: Someone who provokes others online.
Origin: Slang

118."Boomer"
Meaning: An older person who is out of touch.
Origin: Slang

119."Try-hard"
Meaning: Someone who overexerts effort in an unnecessary way.
Origin: Slang

120."Cuffed"
Meaning: Being in a relationship.
Origin: Slang

121."Edgelord"
Meaning: Someone who tries too hard to be edgy or controversial.
Origin: Slang

122."Receipts"
Meaning: Proof of something happening.
Origin: Slang

123."Hypebeast"
Meaning: Someone who only buys trendy brands.
Origin: Streetwear/Hip-Hop Culture

124."Fam"
Meaning: Close friends or family
Origin: Slang

125."Glow-up"
Meaning: A major positive transformation.
Origin: Slang

126."Hits different"
Meaning: Something that feels unique or impactful.
Origin: Slang

127."NPC"
Meaning: Someone who acts predictably, like a background character.
Origin: Slang

128."Manspreading"
Meaning: Sitting with legs too wide, taking up space.
Origin: Slang

129."Heated"
Meaning: Being extremely mad or upset.
Origin: Slang

130."TMI"
Meaning: Too much information.
Origin: Slang

131."Shooketh"
Meaning: A more dramatic version of 'shook'.
Origin: Slang

132."Aesthetic"
Meaning: A visually pleasing or stylish look.
Origin: Slang

133."Viral"
Meaning: Something spreading rapidly online.

134."Savage"
Meaning: Being brutally honest or tough.
Origin: Slang

135."Hundo P"
Meaning: 100% certain or guaranteed.
Origin: Slang

136."Bussin'"
Meaning: Something really good or tasty.
Origin: AAVE/TikTok

137."ICYMI"
Meaning: In case you missed it.
Origin: Slang

138."TFW"
Meaning: That feeling when...
Origin: Slang

139."OK Boomer"
Meaning: Dismissive remark toward outdated opinions.
Origin: Slang

140."Deadass"
Meaning: Completely serious.
Origin: Slang

141."Slaps"
Meaning: Something really good or enjoyable.
Origin: Slang

142."Boomerang"
Meaning: A short looping video, popular on Instagram
Origin: Instagram

143."DM"
Meaning: Direct message.
Origin: Slang

144."Shady"
Meaning: Acting suspicious or untrustworthy.
Origin: Slang

145."IRL"
Meaning: In real life.
Origin: Slang

146."Hundo P"
Meaning: One hundred percent certain.
Origin: Slang

147."Lurking"
Meaning: Watching but not engaging in an online conversation.
Origin: Slang

148."TL;DR"
Meaning: Too long; didn't read.
Origin: Slang

149."Hits different"
Meaning: Something that feels special or unique.
Origin: Slang

150."Throw hands"
Meaning: To start a.
Origin: Slang fight

151."This ain't it, chief"
Meaning: Disapproval of something.
Origin: Slang

152."I'm weak"
Meaning: Something is really funny.
Origin: Slang

153."Swerve"
Meaning: To dodge or avoid something.
Origin: AAVE/Hip-Hop Culture

154."Ratio"
Meaning: A reply getting more engagement than the original post.
Origin: Slang

155."Noob"
Meaning: A newbie or beginner.
Origin: Slang

156."AFK"
Meaning: Away from keyboard.
Origin: Slang

157."Glizzy"
Meaning: A hot dog.
Origin: Slang

158."Womp womp"
Meaning: Expressing disappointment.
Origin: Slang

159."Sheeple"
Meaning: People who blindly follow trends or beliefs.
Origin: Slang

160."Boomer"
Meaning: A dismissive term for older generations
Origin: Slang

161."Bricked up"
Meaning: Feeling excited or aroused.
Origin: Slang

162. "Stan"
Meaning: Obsessive fan behavior.
Origin: Slang

163. "For the culture"
Meaning: Doing something to support or represent a culture.
Origin: Slang

164. "Flexing"
Meaning: Showing off wealth or status.
Origin: Slang

165. "Throwback"
Meaning: A nostalgic reference.
Origin: Slang

166. "Ate and left no crumbs"
Meaning: Did something flawlessly.
Origin: Slang

167. "Basic"
Meaning: Liking mainstream things.
Origin: Slang

168. "Shipped"
Meaning: Wanting two people to be in a relationship.
Origin: Fandom Culture/Tumblr

169. "Thicc"
Meaning: A curvy body type.

170. "Thirst trap"
Meaning: A social media post meant to attract attention.
Origin: Slang

171."Wild"
Meaning: Crazy or unbelievable.
Origin: Slang

172."Pull up"
Meaning: To arrive at a place.
Origin: Slang

173."Receipts"
Meaning: Proof of something happening.
Origin: Slang

174."Drip check"
Meaning: Checking out someone's outfit.
Origin: Hip-Hop Culture

175."Cringe"
Meaning: Something embarrassing or awkward.
Origin: Slang

176."Wig snatched"
Meaning: Being amazed or shocked.
Origin: LGBTQ+/Drag Culture

177."Rizzed up"
Meaning: Flirting successfully.
Origin: Slang

178."Sauce"
Meaning: The Source of information.
Origin: Slang

179."Spill the tea"
Meaning: To gossip.
Origin: Slang

180."Viral moment"
Meaning: Something becoming an internet sensation.
Origin: Slang

181."Weird flex but okay"
Meaning: A strange way of showing off.
Origin: Slang

182."Caught in 4K"
Meaning: Getting caught doing something bad with clear proof.
Origin: Slang

183."Hot take"
Meaning: An unpopular opinion.
Origin: Slang

184."Sussy"
Meaning: Suspicious.
Origin: Slang

185."Clowning"
Meaning: Acting foolishly.
Origin: Slang

186."Doomposting"
Meaning: Constantly posting negative thoughts.
Origin: Slang

187."Zaddy"
Meaning: An attractive older man.
Origin: Slang

188."Litty"
Meaning: Very fun or exciting.
Origin: Slang

189."Vaxxed and waxed"
Meaning: Ready to socialize post-pandemic.
Origin: Slang

190."Slept on"
Meaning: Underrated or not given enough credit.
Origin: Slang

191."Rage quit"
Meaning: Leaving a game or situation out of frustration.
Origin: Slang

192."WYA"
Meaning: Where you at?
Origin: Slang

193."Hit different"
Meaning: Something unique or impactful.
Origin: Slang

194."On fleek"
Meaning: Looking perfect.
Origin: Slang

195."Sending me"
Meaning: Something is hilarious.
Origin: Slang

196."Soft girl era"
Meaning: Embracing femininity and self care.
Origin: Slang

197."Zero chill"
Meaning: Having no restraint or filter.
Origin: Slang

198."Core memory"
Meaning: A significant or nostalgic moment.
Origin: Slang

199."Gassed up"
Meaning: Overly hyped or excited.
Origin: Hip-Hop Culture

200."Outta pocket"
Meaning: Saying something inappropriate.
Origin: Slang

Index

achievements, 23, 24

achievements., 23, 24, 26, 204

ambition, 23, 27, 141, 200

character, 141

conversation, iii, 134, 266

courage, 31, 35

discipline, 165, 207

doubt, 170

doubts, 26, 113

Education, 103, 104, 105, 106, 107, 109, 110, 200, 203

ego, iii

emotion, 122, 184, 253

emotions, 119, 125, 135, 147, 182, 197, 199

experience, 36, 47, 113, 120, 126, 138, 139, 142, 155, 161, 162, 183, 184, 198, 240

failure, 10, 23, 26, 27, 59, 62, 63, 81, 101, 112, 115, 116, 150, 160, 165, 188, 206, 262

Family, 38, 39, 40, 41, 42, 43, 44, 45, 220

Fear, 35, 101, 112, 114, 115, 116, 117, 185, 199, 250, 255

forgiveness, 171, 190

Freedom, 166, 168, 198, 211, 225

friendship, 40, 46, 47, 49, 50, 52, 53, 54, 55, 121, 125

friendships, 38, 39, 40, 46, 49, 50, 52, 53

gain, 4, 113, 128, 135, 176

habit, 65

habits, 5, 65, 68, 73, 145

happiness, 17, 19, 40, 41, 42,
  50, 51, 53, 66, 70, 121, 125,
  135, 187, 206, 209

Honesty, 1, 87, 88, 89, 90, 92,
  93, 94, 171

honor, 91, 190

humility, 65

improvement, 1, 22

Integrity, 87, 88, 91, 92, 93, 94,
  114

intelligence, 105, 106

Justice, 170, 171, 172, 175,
  254

knowledge, iv, 103, 105, 106,
  107, 108, 109, 110, 138, 208,
  260

leadership, 108, 148, 169

Learning, 22, 103, 104, 105,
  106, 107, 108, 110, 142

Life, 29, 30, 31, 32, 33, 34, 35,
  49, 52, 73, 76, 78, 101, 118,
  138, 191, 198, 200, 216,
  223, 225, 228

listening, iii, 106, 183, 204

loss, 26, 32, 63, 262

love, ii, iv, 4, 15, 20, 25, 30,
  33, 35, 36, 38, 39, 41, 42,
  43, 44, 45, 50, 53, 56, 57,
  58, 70, 119, 120, 121, 122,
  123, 124, 125, 163, 191,
  196, 198, 200, 218, 225,
  236, 247, 248

mark, 165

marriage, 157

money, 4, 7, 14, 15, 16, 17, 18,
  19, 20, 40, 56, 59, 66, 69,
  76, 128, 153, 191, 202, 213,
  217

Motivation, 176, 177, 211

Motivational, 23

Opportunity, 24, 204

Pain, 96

Patience, 9, 73, 77, 79, 84, 207

people, iii, 1, 3, 4, 5, 8, 9, 21,
29, 31, 47, 49, 54, 62, 80,
84, 85, 87, 92, 93, 95, 96,
97, 98, 101, 113, 115, 124,
125, 126, 143, 150, 157,
164, 182, 188, 191, 195,
199, 202, 206, 213, 214,
216, 226, 236, 268

Philosophy, 8, 29, 165, 187

power, 19, 98, 99, 100, 103,
113, 116, 119, 143, 163, 167,
168, 181, 195, 196, 201,
226, 241

Pride, 188, 196

progress, 78, 106, 159, 186,
200

purpose, 30, 34, 49, 82, 121,
243

Religion, 188

reputation, 60, 90, 93, 154

Reputation, 88, 94, 190

respect, 45

responsibility, 192

reward, 59, 106, 142

rewards, iii, 9, 22, 24, 56, 57,
82, 139

risk, 2, 4, 10, 24, 127, 150,
159, 181, 206

risks, 19, 22, 35, 58, 80, 81, 82,
99, 105, 111, 112, 137, 141,
202

self, 66, 71, 86, 93, 116, 139,
171, 174, 271

shame, 87, 171, 213

society, 59, 170, 172, 207

strength, 23, 31, 32, 41, 77, 95,
96, 97, 98, 99, 102, 112, 113,
115, 116, 164, 193, 198, 200,
205

struggle, 15, 57, 96, 115, 195,
197

success, 5, 11, 17, 19, 20, 22,
23, 24, 25, 26, 27, 28, 33,
45, 56, 57, 58, 59, 60, 61,
62, 63, 65, 75, 80, 81, 82,
84, 85, 86, 95, 96, 102, 103,

112, 115, 117, 133, 136, 145, 146, 155, 176, 179, 180, 187, 202, 203, 204, 205, 209, 210, 211, 212, 215, 262

suffer, 9, 30, 31, 166, 188

suffering, 30, 199

Suffering, 96

Thinking, 241

time, 157, 160, 177

Time, 68

times, 24, 35, 46, 47, 50, 52, 88, 95, 96, 97, 99, 113, 117, 133, 134, 141, 161, 195, 197, 200, 209

traditional, 82, 83, 136

truth, 1, 12, 50, 53, 87, 88, 89, 90, 91, 92, 93, 164, 171, 173, 189, 196, 216, 228, 239

values, 43

virtue, 94

wealth, 17, 20, 65, 66, 68, 81, 88, 110, 143, 154, 190, 202, 206, 213, 268

Wisdom, 7, 34, 41, 44, 104, 106, 110, 171, 183, 202, 203, 204, 205, 206, 207, 208

work, 3, 4, 18, 22, 23, 25, 26, 27, 56, 57, 58, 59, 60, 63, 70, 78, 79, 80, 83, 86, 107, 133, 161, 176, 186, 211

www.ingramcontent.com/pod-product-compliance
Lightning Source LLC
Chambersburg PA
CBHW070800280326
41934CB00012B/2993